My Son Wears Heels

Harry, age 20, 2011

MY SON WEARS HEELS

One Mom's Journey
from Clueless to Kickass

JULIE TARNEY

Foreword by
Diane Ehrensaft

The University of Wisconsin Press

The University of Wisconsin Press
1930 Monroe Street, 3rd Floor
Madison, Wisconsin 53711-2059
uwpress.wisc.edu

3 Henrietta Street, Covent Garden
London WCE 8LU, United Kingdom
eurospanbookstore.com

Printed in the United States of America

This book may be available in a digital edition.

Library of Congress Cataloging-in-Publication Data

Names: Tarney, Julie, author. | Ehrensaft, Diane, writer of foreword.
Title: My son wears heels: one mom's journey from clueless to kickass / Julie Tarney;
foreword by Diane Ehrensaft.
Description: Madison, Wisconsin: The University of Wisconsin Press, [2016]
| Includes bibliographical references.
Identifiers: LCCN 2016012942 | ISBN 9780299310608 (cloth: alk. paper)
Subjects: LCSH: Tarney, Julie. | Parents of sexual minority youth—Biography.
| Mothers—Biography. | Transgender children—Biography.
Classification: LCC HQ77.8.T37 A3 2016 | DDC 306.874—dc23
LC record available at https://lccn.loc.gov/2016012942

This work is a memoir. It reflects the author's present recollections of her experiences over a period of years. Some names and identifying details have been changed, and certain individuals are composites. Dialogue and events have been recreated from memory, and in some cases chronology has been sparingly compressed or rearranged for the benefit of narrative clarity.

To Harry—my beacon

Contents

Harry James, almost two years old

Foreword

Diane Ehrensaft

When a baby is born, a mystery becomes a reality, but reality also opens up mysteries, some totally unforeseen. And so it is for any baby born with a clear M or F stamped on their birth certificate. Already, before the baby is born, eager observers query, "Girl or boy, do you know yet?" And before that baby even exits the birth canal, a pile of baby presents might pile up in the baby's new room— little pink dresses for girls, little miniature motorcycle jackets for boys. If the letter on that birth certificate is M, we imagine a future of roughhousing, Little League games, darts, or bows-and-arrows. If the letter is F, we envision tea parties, ballet lessons, and baby dolls and dollhouses. These gender-binary images have been imbued in our own growth from birth to maturity.

Such fantasies can be expected in a culture that has clearly divided scripts for boys and for girls. But not all fantasies come true; fantasies of our children's gender may well not. We think their gender is carved in stone as soon as the doctor, nurse, or midwife announces to the parents of the newborn, "You have a beautiful baby girl" or "You have a handsome baby boy." But until that wonderful little baby grows a little (or a lot) and comes to tell us who they are, we can never be so sure about either the gender they know themselves to be or how they prefer to "do" their gender. You may have a son who begs for ballet lessons, a daughter who demands acceptance on the local Little League team, a son who says he's actually your daughter, or a daughter who says she's actually your son. Time will tell. And if you're fast-forwarding to their adult years, forget about wedding cakes with a miniature bride and groom on top. Who your child grows up to love will be a mystery yet to unfold—maybe the cake will have two grooms, or two brides. Again, time will tell.

In *My Son Wears Heels*, Julie Tarney is not going to take us on a sentimental journey but rather an incredible gender journey. She will teach us what it's like to discover that gender is not written in stone and that you could have a son who loves high-heeled shoes— a lot. She doesn't do it through lessons and lectures, but through a moving and poignant account of her life as a mother raising a fabulous, gender creative child.

Little boy, what is your gender? How are you going to "do" your gender? Julie's son, Harry, takes Julie on a challenging and some-times difficult ride as she tries to answer these questions to and about her little boy who plays with girls, loves dress-up, never wants to be the father but always the mother in "Let's play house." So if Harry likes to dress up in dresses, is he gay? Could he be trans? Could he be confused? Could he just be Harry?

Foreword

My Son Wears Heels is going to give you answers to these questions, by allowing us to peer into Julie Tarney's life as a loving mother to her exquisite son, Harry. A long time ago, I grew up to be a feminist of the 1960s. Looking back on that time, we all thought we were kicking up some dust, and we were happy for it. We had no idea we had started a landslide, earthshaking tremors that would set in motion, with the aid of our allies in the LGBTQI movement, a new era in which homosexuality would be deleted as a mental disorder in the Diagnostic Statistical Manual (1973), gay marriage would be legalized in the United States (2015), and reparative therapy to try to "fix" the gender or sexual identity of minors would be banned in several states in the United States and a province in Canada. Many of us are mesmerized by the seemingly sudden breakdown of the gender binary—one box for boys and one box for girls, and never the twain shall meet. When even Target stores dispense with gender categories in their toy departments (which they announced in the summer of 2015), we are definitely in a whole new world. As the twenty-first century rolls on, we are bearing witness to an explosion in the acknowledgment, understanding, and celebration of people of all genders and sexualities. Gender used to be bedrock, and now we've converted it into moving boulders. Marriage used to be the sole providence of a man and a woman, and I should add as a man and a woman who started out that way. Now we recognize marriage as the loving union between two people of any gender and any sexual identity. It is in this terrain that Julie Tarney birthed her book, *My Son Wears Heels: One Mom's Journey from Clueless to Kickass*. How can we make sense of her remarkable journey with her son, Harry?

Some Reading Guidelines

I've been working as a psychologist and gender specialist for many years now. I'm also the mom of two grown children, both of whom loved tutus—one my daughter, the other my son. As they grew up I discovered that one is straight, the other gay. With that said, from my vantage point as both a professional and a mother, I want to offer you some reading guidelines as you embark on Julie Tarney's wonderful excursion in *My Son Wears Heels*. I'm going to share with you what I've put together as a roadmap for adults in following children's journeys as they consolidate their gender selves and their sexual being.

A three-year-old boy shows up in a princess costume. A common response (if you're lucky): "How cute. Do you think he's gay?" Herein lies our first reading guideline: Sexual identity (gay, straight, queer, pansexual, and so forth) is a completely separate developmental track from gender identity and expression. In adult parlance, if this helps—sexual identity is who you go to bed with; gender identity is who you go to bed as. The three-year-old boy wearing a princess dress may indeed grow up to be gay, as many gender-nonconforming children do. But that three-year-old might also be one of our transgender children, eager to let us know that he is not the gender we think he is. Or he may just be a child who likes to break gender boundaries, without changing the sex marked on his birth certificate and with no reflection at all on his future sexual identity. All we know is that we have a three-year-old child who loves to dress up in lace and frills. Where this will go only he knows, as long as no one tries to stop him. So, first guideline: think of gender and sexuality as if they were two separate sets of railroad tracks, running parallel to each other but sometimes crisscrossing, as when "protogay" children explore and transcend the culturally defined margins of gender on their way to discovering their sexual identities.

In our developmental theories, we posit that children will be aware of their gender long before they are aware of their sexuality. So let's stay in early childhood for now, when children are learning about, exploring, and discovering gender—their own and others' around them—but not yet formulating their sexual identities. They do not do this in a vacuum, but in the context of the world they were born into—with a certain set of parents and siblings, in a certain town or city, in a certain country, with a particular set of values attached. To explain how this unfolds, let me introduce you to my personal construction: the gender web. Once a child is born, every single baby will have a job ahead of them—to weave together their own gender web. The gender web is a four-dimensional structure. If we imagine it in space, the gender web will be constructed from three major categories of threads—nature, nurture, and culture. Nature is what we are born with and what is in our bodies—our chromosomes, our hormones, our brains, our minds, our organs. Nurture is the people who raise us—our parents, our extended families, our childcare providers, our teachers. Culture is the social context in which all that nurturing occurs—our religions, our values, our ethics, our laws, our beliefs.

Like fingerprints, no two children's gender webs will be alike. Each child will weave their own unique gender web. That's true for you and me as well, as adults. But unlike fingerprints, which will remain exactly the same from the day you are born to the day you die, our gender webs can change over the course of our lives, engaging the fourth dimension: time. Just as Rome wasn't built in a day, so it is with the gender web. It takes time to put together and it is not indelible. The gender web we spun at age three may look very different from the one we're working on at age twenty-five, or forty, or sixty. So spinning a gender web is a lifelong process that can evolve over time. And it takes a lot of creativity, which is what made me coin the term "gender creativity." By definition, gender creativity is the process of weaving together your own unique gender web, pulling together over time all those different threads that are part of the other three dimensions—nature, nurture, and culture. Some children will weave together a gender web that looks very "regular" or conforming, just like we expect a boy or girl to look, by cultural standards. Other children will draw far outside the lines, ignoring the boundaries set by the culture around them on how to "do" gender. These will be our most gender creative children, and you will be introduced to one as you learn about Harry through Julie's eyes.

Which brings me to the question of parents. Where do parents fit into the gender web? The gender web is the child's own special creation. If parents step in to put their own stamp on it, they will only leave their child all tangled up in knots about their gender. That mess happens every time a parent says to a little boy who loves his sister's baby doll, "Honey, that doll's not for you because you're a boy and boys don't play with dolls." It happens every time a little boy comes to his mother and says, "Mommy, I'm not a boy. Everybody's got it wrong, I'm actually a girl," and the mother says,

"Honey, it's you who has it wrong. You're a boy because you have a penis, and girls can't have penises. So let's just drop that silly notion." If, instead of stepping in, parents step back and create a safe and loving space for their child to spin their own unique gender web, the child feels expansive, accepted, and delighted in the web they have put together. That celebratory moment happens every time a mother says to her son, "Of course you can have a baby doll. Your friend Alex was just confused when he teased you that dolls are only for girls. Dolls are for people, and you're a person, aren't you?" It happens every time a mother says to her son, "Oh, my. Tell me more about getting it wrong. I know we thought you were a boy, but maybe we were mistaken. Does your inside tell you that you're a girl?" From my perspective, being gender creative is what we want for our children. And this is where parents come in. It takes a gender creative parent to raise a gender creative child. It takes a gender-rejecting parent to crush a child's gender zest. So here we see the second dimension in play: nurture.

And of course, we can't forget about the world beyond the parent—the cultural threads of the gender web, the third dimension. Not everybody embraces the gender creative child. Not everybody looks kindly on the gender creative parent. So to negotiate a world that may not always be friendly to gender-nonconforming or gay or queer people, children and parents alike will have to learn how to build their gender resilience, defined as the ability to stand up with pride in the child's gender creativity, regardless of what anyone else thinks. I'm thinking of an eight-year-old boy who wore his pink sparkly butterfly shirt to school. An older fifth-grader came up to him, wrinkled up his nose, and belted out, "You can't wear a pink shirt. Only girls wear pink!" And our little eight-year-old responded, quite calmly, "Well, I'm a boy. And I'm wearing a pink shirt. So I guess boys can wear pink." That's gender resilience. And now I'm thinking of a mother who accompanied her child, Danny, to the first day of school after Danny transitioned from being a boy to being a girl over the summer, choosing to wear a dress and fancy shoes for this special day. A classmate came running over and screeched to a halt, staring at Danny and then grilling the mom: "Wait a second, I thought Danny was a boy." And the mom stepped right up and explained, "Yeah, so did we. But then we discovered we were wrong. We learned Danny's a girl." That's gender resilience, executed by a mom on behalf of her child. And I should add that once the issue was clarified, this little classmate was delighted to discover her new girlfriend, as the two skipped off together to the playground. These are not isolated stories. I am witnessing such heartfelt and profound gender resilience every day, as I am fortunate to get to know so many gender creative children and their families. It is this very gender resilience that we will witness passing back and forth between Julie and Harry, mother and son, as Julie unfolds her story of raising her son who wears high heels in a world that does not always look so kindly on that.

So let me summarize the reader's guidelines:

- Gender and Sexuality as Two Separate Tracks
- The Gender Web and Its Four Dimensions
- Gender Creativity
- Gender Resilience.

I invite you to use any and all of these features as your GPS as you join Julie Tarney on her parental journey from clueless to kickass.

From Blame the Parent to Thank the Mom

As you read through the chapters of *My Son Wears Heels*, always keep in mind the lines from Kahlil Gibran's poem *The Prophet*: "Your children are not your children . . . They come through you but not from you." Translated to our topic, the vast majority of parents who have a child who defies the gender norms of the culture from an early age will tell you something like, "My child just came to me that way. I swear, I did nothing to encourage it. As a matter of fact, I have three other children, and they're all boys' boys or girls' girls. It's just this little one that's breaking all the gender rules. I don't know where she comes from." When it comes to children's gender, my profession, in the field of psychology/mental health, has traditionally paid little heed to the words of Gibran's poem, seeing children not as coming through but being molded by their parents. In short, collectively we have been guilty of blaming parents, particularly mothers, if their son wears heels. A boy likes "girly" things. Mom made it happen by being too involved with her son, keeping him too close to her bosom. Mom didn't stop it, maybe even encouraged it, leaving her child gender disordered and sure to grow up gay—and this is not seen as a good thing but as a thing that could surely be "fixed" through reparative therapy for the child and mental health treatment for the mom. Result: Traditionally, mothers of gender creative children were totally silenced. No mother would ever come forward to tell her story, unless she wanted to be skewered publicly and morally condemned. In that historical light, *My Son Wears Heels* is both transgressive and transcendent. Transgressive, because it defies my profession's misguided tropes on children, gender, sexual identity, and parenting.

Transcendent, because like Black Power, Women's Liberation, Gay Pride, and Rainbow Pride, mothers of gender creative children can now come forward and share their joys, their struggles, their commitment, and their love for their sons who wear heels, their daughters who have buzz cuts, their children who tell them they are not the gender everyone thinks they are, their sons and daughters who declare their sexual identities as gay, lesbian, or queer. As Julie Tarney allows us into the innermost sanctuary of her relationship with Harry, she knows all too well that our gender creative children not only go through us, they teach us as they go.

Dreaming

Let's go back to, "When a baby is born." As parents, we start dreaming about our children before we ever meet them. Before they're born, we can't yet meet them in our waking lives. So we bring them to life at night or when we nap—in our dreams. We close our eyes and let our unconscious draw portraits and create animations. And those dreams don't stop when our children finally enter our lives as real little people. But now they are waking dreams. Most babies don't mind this. As they grow, children like to know that they're important and special enough to enter their parents' dream lives. To a point. Things turn south when parents' dreams dominate children's realities. It is the parent who always dreamed their child would be a piano virtuoso, maybe because they themselves never got a chance. So they send their child to piano lessons and organize scheduled practices every day. The only problem is that their child is dreaming something very different—maybe they want to be an astronaut or a football player or a fashion designer, not a pianist. To have a good go of it, that child needs to claim their own dreams, and the parents need to put theirs to rest. So it is with a child and their gender, and later their sexuality. Both are their own possessions, no one else's. Their dreams for themselves may be totally opposite to the ones their parents have been having for them. Maybe they will be boys who wear heels or girls who love girls, dreaming of the life that will unfold from there.

There is one simple rule to remember when our children come to us in all their gender creativity. These are not our dreams, but theirs. Parents' work is to come to a place where they can embrace all their children's dreams, even when they don't match their own. When it comes to children's gender, I have a saying: "It is not for us to tell, but for the children to say." Our job is to listen, and to stop our own dreams from clouding our vision, thereby losing sight of what our children are trying to show us.

So one three-year-old boy sleeps in his princess dress every night, he loves it so much. He dreams wearing it. He dreams of himself wearing it. In that moment, we don't know if that little boy will be grow up to be gay (which is the stereotypical fallback when we observe a boy who likes to do "girl" things). We don't know if he will discover that he is transgender. We don't know if he'll just be a gender expansive, gender creative person all his life. What we do know right then is that happiness comes with getting to wear his princess dress, and that he is telling something very important about himself, all the while bucking the socially inscribed expectations, prescriptions, and proscriptions that dictate how boys should be and girls should be, if he is even aware of them. At that moment we can't know where the path will lead. Only the child can dream it.

Our job is to let the child take the lead and see where it ends up. As adults, we can put up roadblocks or we can strew rose petals and love as we walk alongside our children on their gender paths.

The task of relinquishing our gender dreams and instead honoring the children's is not always an easy one, and may come with inside contortions and outside snags along the way. Some relationships even fall apart in the process, especially when two parents can't see eye to eye about their child's gender or sexuality. To buttress ourselves during the process, we can just keep repeating this mantra: These are not our dreams, they are our child's dreams.

Compass in Hand, You're Ready for the Journey

If I am your roadmap, then Julie Tarney is your compass, guiding your path, starting on the very first page of the book, when two-year-old Harry questions Julie, "Momma . . . How do you know I'm a boy?" And they are off and running in a wonderful mother-son duo, with us following behind. I won't give away the punch line, but suffice it to say that you are headed for a wonderful treat as Julie Tarney invites us to come along on her journey from birth to maturity with Harry, as she moves as a parent from "clueless to kickass," never leaving her son's side for a moment as he carves his path with her support. As you read, you will also witness a little boy growing up weaving his own gender web as he goes, in the most creative of ways, affirming both his gender self and his sexual identity. Harry doesn't just wear heels, he challenges us to rethink all of our stereotypes of boy, girl, man, woman, who they are, and who they love. And all the while, Julie Tarney provides the voice-over of what it is like to be the mother on the journey.

Foreword

When I was a child, I loved to watch *Hit Parade* (I divulge my age here). Every week I waited for them to sing, "When I was just a little girl / I asked my mother, 'What will I be? / Will I be pretty, will I be rich?' / Here's what she said to me, / 'Que sera, sera. / Whatever will be, will be. / The future's not ours to see. / Que sera, sera.'" And then Doris Day was singing it every day on the radio. "Will I be pretty?" was a trope offered to any girl growing up in America, still is. But if I were to change the words to fit the changing terrain of twenty-first-century life with our moving boulders of gender, children may be asking their mothers, and fathers as well, "Will I be female?" "Will I be male?" "Will I be straight?" "Will I be gay?," and their mothers, and fathers, will croon, with love, acceptance, and anticipation, "Que sera, sera. / Whatever will be, will be." And I can hear Julie Tarney as the lead singer.

Diane Ehrensaft, PhD, is a developmental and clinical psychologist. At the University of California–San Francisco, she is the cofounder and director of mental health at the Child and Adolescent Gender Center, an associate professor of pediatrics, and an attending psychologist at the Benioff Children's Hospital Child and Adolescent Gender Clinic. She is the author of several books, including *Gender Born, Gender Made: Raising Healthy Gender-Nonconforming Children* (2011) and *The Gender Creative Child: Pathways for Nurturing and Supporting Children Who Live Outside Gender Boxes* (2016). Her work with—and advocacy for—gender creative children has been widely covered, including by *The New York Times* and NPR. She has appeared on *Anderson*, *The Oprah Winfrey Show*, and *The Today Show*.

My Son Wears Heels

July 4th at Crystal Lake, Wisconsin

Ken Hanson

How Do You Know
I'm a Boy?

Harry whooshed past me, sputtering his own version of airborne sound effects. He jumped into the slew of stuffed toy animals that lined his bottom bunk bed and rolled up onto his knees. I watched him pat first his left shoulder, then the right, making sure the Velcro tabs of his red cape were still attached to the top of his size 2T Superman pajamas. He sat up and put his barefoot soles together on the sea of bright-colored Mickey Mouse heads that patterned his quilt.

I sat in the middle of Harry's bedroom carpet in a laundry-folding reverie. Aside from the whir of air blowing through the AC vent in the ceiling, the house was quiet. His tie-dyed t-shirts and bandana shorts made by a friend at work were still warm from the dryer. I breathed in laundry freshness mingled with the scent of watermelon kids shampoo and felt comforted by the hominess of this before-bedtime solitude. After an intense all-day client meeting, I was ready to kick back and relax during some welcome alone time.

Harry watched me, and his right thumb and forefinger played with what he called the "flippy piece" edge of his "lamby," a lamb-skin-wool baby blanket. He was waiting for something.

"Momma?" he finally said, tentatively.

"Yes, Harry?"

"How do you know I'm a boy?"

I looked up. What brought that on? Why wasn't he asking me what book we were going to read? Then I remembered that the son of a friend was two when he wanted to know why girls had two butts, so I figured this was an age-appropriate question. I decided to stick to the basics.

"Well, honey," I said, clearing my throat. "Boys have a penis and girls have a vagina. You have a penis."

Harry tilted his head of downy blond curls and I recognized his pose—he was processing the information. A few days earlier he and his neighborhood posse of Billy, Allison, and Travis had spent an afternoon running naked through the backyard sprinkler, so I thought maybe he was verifying my answer with a playback of that outdoor scene.

But as I stacked the last of his brightly colored socks in spectrum order, I noticed Harry's expression shift to a "Hmm." Then, holding his feet, he rocked back and squinted. I could tell he was sorting through ideas. I wondered what it was about my answer that was making him think this hard. Maybe he wanted to say something and was trying to figure out how to say it. I decided to probe a little.

"That was an interesting question, Harry. What made you think of it?"

"Well, inside my head I'm a girl."

"Oh," I responded, with an air of upbeat acknowledgment. Now I was the one processing. He was so matter-of-fact, so self-assured in his reply.

Harry's blue eyes were staring straight at me and it seemed as if the eyes of all his stuffed animals were fixed on me, too. Stalling for time, I slowly rolled up my small frame and smiled. In the few seconds it took to go from seated and stunned to upright and uptight, my brain speed-scanned every "How to Talk to Your Child About . . ." article I kept stashed in a folder at work. As the marketing agency for OshKosh B'Gosh, we subscribed to every parenting magazine, so I began clipping articles for future reference as soon as I knew I was pregnant. But I couldn't recall anything that would help me in this moment. My head was throbbing and I wasn't sure I was breathing. I wanted to be Glinda, the Good Witch of the North, who would have just the right answer.

"Well, it's a good thing you know that about yourself, Harry."

He rocked back and flashed a wide, baby-toothed grin. I could hear the game show host of *Family Feud* praising me with an enthusiastic "Good answer!"

God Bless America.

After story time with Frog and Toad, a few verses of my made-up Little Kitty lullaby, goodnight kisses, and lights out, I left Harry's door open a crack and stood motionless outside his room. My thoughts were back in Speed Racer mode. I recapped the scene. "Inside my head I'm a girl." I knew what it meant, but what did it *mean*?

Maybe Harry was trying to tell me he was a girl in a boy's body. Or possibly he was giving me the heads-up he was gay without even knowing the concept. Then I wondered if that's what famous transsexual Christine Jorgensen told her mother when she was two years old. It was 1992, and she was my only reference for someone who'd undergone a sex-change operation. I didn't know much about people who identified as a gender different from the one assigned to them at birth and I figured most people knew even less. Rock Hudson's death from AIDS was the prevailing image of homosexuality; being gay was a stigma and a pandemic. I wasn't sure what any of this meant for me or for Harry.

I walked straight to the shelves in the guest bedroom and scanned our small collection of parenting books, all bought two years earlier after a blue plus sign appeared on my at-home pee test. My forefinger brushed over the spines of the retired volumes of *What to Expect When You're Expecting* and *What to Expect the First Year*. Where was *What to Expect When Your Two-Year-Old Comes Out to You*?

I settled on *Dr. Spock's Baby and Child Care*. It was a fifth edition paperback of the only parenting book my mother considered an essential reference for new moms. "It's like the Bible," she insisted in fourth grade when my teacher was going on maternity leave and I wanted to buy her a present. Even though my mother was dead, I heard her peremptory voice saying I'd be sorry if I were pregnant and didn't have Spock's book. While I'd rebelled against her advice even into adulthood and didn't want to be anything like her, I figured Dr. Spock was a known expert and maybe had some insight.

I tucked my wavy chestnut hair behind my ears, searched the index for "sexuality," and found an entry for "homosexuality."

6

"See!" I heard my mother say. The memory of her dictatorial tone was sharp enough to pick the lock on a fear I'd hoped to bury after her death: The possibility that I could become like her. I surely didn't want to read about any of the theories that controlling mothers were the cause of homosexuality in boys. I hesitated turning to the page; in some ways I *was* controlling and I didn't want to be condemned.

It was true that no two colors of my Fiestaware plates or bowls touched each other in their stacks. My knife drawer was organized from largest to smallest. My husband Ken teased that if he got up at night to use the bathroom I'd make his side of the bed. He even joked to friends I was so obsessively clean that I'd put a coat of Mop & Glo on the driveway after shoveling snow. I knew I color-coordinated Harry's sock drawer, made sure his fingers were never sticky, and left five pages of detailed, typed-up notes for his baby-sitters. But that wasn't the same as my mother telling me not to touch my face or to close my mouth when I breathed.

I sank onto the guest room bed, found the page, and then wondered why I bothered to sit down at all. What the hell? There were only two measly paragraphs.

In the first one, Doc Spock said the majority of what he referred to as "feminine boys" and "masculine boys" grow up to be hetero-sexual. The next paragraph was longer. I read it and then reread it. Spock gave a few hypotheticals, which I understood. But it was his overuse of certain adverbs that threw me off. I was stumped by the absolutes of *only*, *exclusively*, and *always*.

According to the good doctor, if Harry wanted to dress *exclusively* in girl clothes and play *only* with girls, he might have some of his ideas mixed up. And if he wanted to play *only* with girls and was *always* unhappy about his biological gender, I might want to consult with a child psychiatrist. But if the dress and play activities occurred only *occasionally*, the door was still open for Harry to join the hetero majority.

I wanted Harry surrounded by the safety and protection of large numbers on the school playground. I fast-forwarded to him as a gay adult not being able to get married, or have kids, or keep the job he loved. I thought of my close childhood friend in Los Angeles who was dying of AIDS. I would never wish for my son to be gay. I took a deep yoga breath in and exhaled slowly.

Spock's unspoken words were: if after age five or six the "only-exclusively-always" modifiers predominated, it was time to schedule an appointment with a shrink.

"Huh!" I thought. I'm supposed to wait until Harry is five or six to know what's going on? What about now? What about the next three or four years? What about Harry's next question or surprise statement? I studied those two paragraphs several times, and then put a purple sticky tab on the page. At least there was no mention of controlling mothers. Still, I decided I liked Dr. Spock better as a peace activist.

I recounted the whole story to Ken when he got home from a dinner meeting.

"What does that mean?" he asked.

"I have no idea what it means!"

I read aloud to him what little the Spock book offered.

His face twisted in puzzlement. "That doesn't tell us much now, does it?"

"No," I said. "It says nothing. And who takes a happy, confident kid to a shrink anyway?"

"Well, we're definitely not doing that."

"But what *do* we do?"

"We don't have to do anything. He's two."

"Really? Nothing? Don't you think Harry was revealing something kind of heavy?"

"Julie, he's two. Let's just see how it goes."

I didn't say another word. Maybe Ken was right. Our differences had found a sweet spot the summer we met in 1978. He was Beatles, I was Stones. He was mountains, I was beach. He ran, I did yoga. He didn't believe in astrology, I read my daily horoscope. He was the glass half full that filled mine up with positivity. I needed his inborn patience now to balance my natural compulsiveness as my mind stayed in overdrive.

I wondered if I had missed any earlier signs from Harry. I flashed back a few months to the day he asked my dad and stepmother a question that seemed to come out of nowhere.

Our pint-sized comic Harry scrunched his face as he squatted in front of the living room couch to smell my father's sock-covered feet. "Eww," Harry said, pinching his nose as he stood up. "Stinky feet!"

It was two weeks before his second birthday, and Harry had created this new bit of toddler entertainment with his twenty-two-year-old nanny, Heidi. Ken and I had laughed a few days earlier when our feet were first declared stinky, but I wasn't so sure how my dad and stepmother would take the news.

Grandpa Don's blue eyes widened as he exploded his staccato laughter, and, encouraged, Harry bounced across the room to the blue leather chair occupied by Grandma Fran, where he gave a repeat performance.

"Oh my!" Fran said, blushing the color of her rescue-squad-red turtleneck sweater. She tousled Harry's curls while my father roared again. Harry bounded back to the couch and landed between Ken and my dad.

"You are such a nutcase, Harry," Ken teased.

"Do you know what a nutcase is, Harry?" I asked.

"Yes, it's like a suitcase, but for nuts."

His audience of four chuckled.

"It means a little kooky or wacky, and funny," Ken said.

Harry slid off the couch to twirl in the middle of the rug. When he stopped he was facing Fran.

"Do you know the difference between men and women?" Harry asked.

Fran winked at me, amused.

"No, Harry-who-lives-on-Hackett," she answered. "Tell us, what is the difference?"

I turned from the stereo cabinet to exchange raised eyebrows with Ken. I had no idea where that question came from and couldn't imagine what Harry's answer would be. He took occasional baths with Ken and had walked in on me in the bathroom a few times, so my silent guess was "boobs."

Harry laced his fingers and held his arms straight out.

"Earrings!" he said, with a little jump.

"Well, yes, I guess that is a difference," Fran conceded.

As Harry walked up to examine the large gold knot designs that hung from Fran's earlobes, she shot a quick glance in my direction, apparently unsure if she should say more. Instead she took off her earring for Harry to look at more closely.

As I lay in bed later next to a snoring Ken, who clearly didn't think Harry's pronouncement was any big deal, I felt panicked and couldn't sleep. I flipped through recent memories for more missed clues. And then came the nagging thought that Harry's confusion was somehow my fault. Maybe if I wasn't so manic and controlling and overprotective. When Harry was born partially blind in one eye, the pediatric ophthalmologist told me Harry would need to wear glasses without a prescription just to protect his good eye. That warning turned me into a vigilante. "No playing with sticks, ever!" I told babysitters. I decided Tinker Toys would be banned. I wore nonprescription glasses over my contact lenses and asked Heidi to do the same, thinking Harry would want to wear his glasses if we wore them, too. I knew I was being overprotective, but I couldn't back off from keeping Harry's good eye safe. I wondered if I'd made the wrong call. Maybe I should have been more lax.

In the weeks that followed Harry's "inside my head" statement I spent a lot of time inside my own head trying to understand my two-year-old son. I wondered if it had anything to do with the fact that his friend Billy's older sister Natalie didn't allow the two of them to touch her Barbie dolls or play with her Barbie Dream House in their attic playroom across the street.

I knew from Billy's mom that the two boys were regularly in trouble over there for sneaking into Natalie's Barbies. Was it the plastic blonde's off-limits status that made her so attractive to Harry? Did he think he might be a girl in his desire for her as a toy?

When Ken and I took Harry on his first outing to Toys R Us to spend the twenty-dollar bill Ken's dad in Florida had sent him in a Fourth of July card, we said he could buy any toy he wanted that didn't cost more than the money from Gramps. Harry passed the first aisle of squirt guns, beach toys, and summer sporting goods with the eagerness of a kid headed downstairs on Christmas morning.

Guided by pink and purple signs, he found his way to the girls toy section and slowed his pace at the doll aisle. He stopped in front of the stacked shelves of Barbies and pointed to a box holding Cinderella Barbie. Ken and I looked at each other with questioning shoulders raised and eyebrows arched.

"Are you sure that's what you want, Harry?" I asked.

He nodded.

"You know, Harry, we haven't even really looked around," Ken said. "There are a lot of toys in here."

Harry's lower lip quivered before he started to jump up and down screaming. It was an instant meltdown, and other shoppers were turning to see what we could possibly be doing to our child. Mortified, Ken reached for Cinderella Barbie, whose box became the magic wand that quickly returned our son to his happy self.

Harry, beaming, wanted to take her out of the packaging right away, but we said he had to wait until we were in the car. It took the entire drive from Toys R Us to K-Mart for me to unfasten the seemingly endless number of thick plastic ties while Harry wriggled in his car seat, impatient to hold his very own Disney princess. The two were still inseparable when my brother Jack came from San Diego to visit us in hometown Milwaukee over Labor Day weekend.

Wearing the new neon pink swim trunks he wore every day and clutching a naked Barbie, Harry ran through the kitchen past Jack and me to the back door. He was headed outside to the hot tub, where Ken and his sister were relaxing before dinner.

Jack rubbed his chin. "Are you *trying* to raise a gay kid?"

I laughed. I knew my brother was joking and not some awful homophobic uncle. Still, I couldn't help but feel like I was being blamed for Harry's love of Barbie. I wasn't going to let Jack try to make a big deal out of it. "What are you talking about?"

"Come on, Julie. A Barbie doll?"

"So what? He wanted it. You had a doll when you were little, too."

"I did?"

"Yeah, you were jealous that June and I had baby dolls to play with when the three of us were in the bath together. So Mother got you one, too."

"Huh. I don't remember that."

I had listened from the other room when my mother called my grandmother, worried about Jack's request for a doll. She didn't think it was a good idea. But Nana must have said it was okay, because Jack got the doll. He only wanted to play with it in the bathtub. And when water didn't squirt out of its butt like my Betsy Wetsy, but only dribbled drops from its belly button, he soon lost interest.

Harry had two plastic wind-up bath dolls of his own when he was a baby, a lookalike boy and girl who swam when their arms spun. The girl swimmer, with a red-and-white polka dot swim cap painted on her head, was Harry's favorite tub toy and soon broke from overuse. Now, after the last two months of watching him play with his Barbie doll, and knowing his best friend Billy liked playing with her, too, I was determined to view Barbie as just another tub doll.

"You know what I think?" Jack asked.

I can't wait.

My brother fancied himself a pop psychologist. He was sure the reason I used to smoke cigarettes was because our mother hadn't nursed me as a baby.

"No, what do you think, Jack?"

"I think Harry's in love with Heidi, and Barbie reminds him of her."

Harry's nanny Heidi was the German version of Barbie, the friend of a friend at work. She was blonde, willowy, and super-model stunning, with the disposition of Julie Andrews in *The Sound of Music.* I thanked my lucky stars for her every morning when I left for work.

"Are you sure *you're* not in love with Heidi and just projecting your fantasies on Harry?"

A corner of Jack's mouth turned up into a half smile. I had busted him, and he knew it.

"Well, feel free to play with Harry's Barbie as your replacement. If he'll part with her, that is." Then I followed Harry's wet footprints out to the back deck, where nude Cinderella Barbie sat in regal splendor on a cup holder built into the edge of the hot tub. She looked like a leader, presiding over the happily splashing subject who adored her. But after defending Harry's prized possession to Jack, I wasn't so sure I trusted her to be my son's leader. I remembered that moment in Toys R Us when Ken and I had exchanged our Harry-wants-a-Barbie look. Was this something I should still be concerned about? Was Barbie going to become Harry's role model?

Before the Halloween block party, 1992

The Toilet Paper Bride

October's witchy winds sent yellow leaves flying from the stretch of mature trees lining our turn-of-the-century city block in Milwaukee. As I looked out the bay window of our living room I thought it ironic that we lived less than a mile from the house where my mother had grown up. In college, I'd always imagined ending up somewhere more cosmopolitan. I spotted two of the Marino kids playing with a ball on their wide front porch. Three doors down in the other direction a large pumpkin cutout hung at street level with a half-row of lace curtains in the Kelly's window. Although their daughters were out of college now, Patrick and Laura Kelly remained the all-holidays weathervane for the three dozen kids living on our block.

I had no idea how lucky Ken and I would be when we started the search for our first home. The realtor's listing description read "perfect for a family" and "lots of kids," but I'd glossed over those so-called benefits. Kids were not on my career-advancing agenda, and Ken was okay with that. What mattered to us was staying on

the East Side, price, and a third-floor attic with remodeling potential. As it turned out, the home with everything we wanted was in
the middle of a street overrun by kids. And not just little kids.
Hackett Avenue was a babysitter goldmine.

As I sipped my coffee, watching neighbors rake their yards and
children jump into leaf piles, I thought about Harry fitting into
this community of kids. I hoped a boy who felt like a girl could be
just one of the gang. Then I thought of Aaron, one of Harry's high-
school-aged babysitters from a few doors down. Aaron was a handsome, talented dancer who just happened to be gay. I wondered if
he'd told his mother he felt like a girl when he was a toddler. But
either way, I knew someone could be creative and straight. Harry's
dad was a designer and fine art photographer, and he wasn't gay.
Oddly though, Aaron seemed a dynamic, androgynous fusion of
masculine and feminine. I wondered if that's what the psychic
meant when she told me three years earlier that Harry would be
like me. Maybe I should have paid more attention to her.

I remembered that Saturday afternoon in July vividly. Ken and I
had just polished off our paper plates of crêpes drizzled with
chocolate sauce at the Bastille Day festival downtown.

"Are you ready?" Ken asked. "Paul Cebar and the Milwaukeeans
are playing at the stage on Kilbourn, and I don't want to miss them."

"Okay," I said, pulling a cigarette from my purse. "But I'll meet
you over there. I want to stop at the Psychic Faire tent near the park
and have my cards read before it gets too crowded."

I was excited to see a short line, but then found out there was a
waiting list on a clipboard. "How long for a tarot card reader?" I
asked the man wearing a beret.

"About half an hour, forty-five minutes tops."

I didn't want to wait that long for a fifteen-minute reading.

"But I do have a psychic astrologer available now," he said.

I hesitated. Today I was eager for quick answers from the cards. But a psychic reading was better than no reading.

I paid the man twelve dollars and took a seat next to a small folding table. A travel clock, some crystals, and a few worn books sat atop a blue tie-dye tablecloth imprinted with signs of the zodiac. A woman who appeared to be in her late forties greeted me with a smile. Her soft features were framed by frizzy strawberry blond hair parted down the middle.

She jotted down my birth date, and asked that I not say anything else. She consulted one of her books and scribbled a few notes. Then she asked to hold my hands. She closed her eyes and didn't speak until she blinked.

"Are you pregnant?" she blurted.

"I-I don't know," I said, startled. "I could be."

Ken and I had stopped using birth control a year after my mother died, but my periods were never regular, so I wasn't sure if I was just late or not. I put my right hand up to my left breast. It did feel a little sore.

"I think you are," said the psychic, "and you're going to have a boy."

I couldn't believe it. Was this really happening? I knew Ken would be happy with either a boy or a girl, but I thought my father-in-law would be delighted to hear our baby was a boy. Neither of his two grandsons shared his surname. Then my palms itched as I felt a rush of fear. I was still haunted by Nancy Friday's 1977 best-seller *My Mother/My Self: The Daughter's Search for Identity*. Her research disclosed that a daughter's feelings of anger and hatred toward her mother could create some sort of motherhood legacy. It was the first time my private nightmare of turning into my mother became public discourse. I shuddered at the time, thinking there might be some inescapable genetic stain that would trigger in me her style of critical parenting and conditional love. Ken understood my fears and went along with the idea of a childless marriage. I never thought I'd have kids, but now that the possibility was imminent, I wondered if I was really ready to be a mother, and a Jewish mother at that.

"No, wait," the psychic said, interrupting my inner mama drama. "It's a girl."

Seriously, lady? You've got a fifty-fifty chance of getting this right. So which is it?

"No," she said, hesitating. "You're having a boy . . . but he's going to be like you."

"Okay . . . ," I replied, unsure I could believe anything she said at this point. I studied her face. There was something sincere about her confused expression that kept me from dismissing her completely. She looked as if the universe was giving her crossed signals for the first time ever.

She had known I was pregnant before I did. When she said I'd have a boy who'd be like me, I assumed she meant dark hair and freckles like me, but neither was true. Trying to piece together past and present, I wondered if somehow she knew there'd be something different about Harry. Had she seen that he'd be both a boy *and* a girl? I was in over my head. I didn't know if I had it in me to be the kind of good, easy-going mother that I thought Harry needed. I didn't know how to manage myself, let alone handle my son who was a self-proclaimed girl.

A few weeks later when I opened the front door to bring in the mail, I wasn't surprised to find an orange flyer with clip art of dancing jack-o-lanterns. It was the lineup of Friday night events that would transform our street into a full-blown costume party.

I beamed, imagining Harry's face when I told him what was coming up. At two and a half, he was now old enough to join the block's Halloween festivities. Last year, he'd spent the day in the orange Alvin and the Chipmunks pajamas that Gramps sent from Florida, topped off with Mickey Mouse ears. The year before that, when he was seven months old, Ken and I had paraded him around in a quilted yellow bunting that doubled as an infant's banana costume.

Now, the colorful flyer in hand, I headed for the living room where Harry was curled up in the blue leather chair watching the cartoon version of *Peter Pan* for what was probably the fourth time in as many days. He loved repeating favorites, whether books or videos, and would ask to hear the same stories over and over again.

"Harry, guess what?" I called out excitedly. "Remember when I told you about the Halloween block party? Well, it's this weekend!" Moving to the TV, I paused the VCR to get his attention, and he looked up at me slowly, his Disney trance broken.

"It's a Halloween party at night! There's trick or treating, a haunted house, scary stories, piñatas, a bonfire and fireworks! And you get to dress up in a costume. You can be anyone you want!"

"Okay, I'll be Wendy."

"Wendy?"

"Yes." He glanced back at the picture, now frozen on the TV screen.

"You mean Wendy from *Peter Pan*?"

Harry nodded with a look that said, "What other Wendy is there?"

I didn't know what to say. I managed a shaky grin, and agreed, "Okay! Wendy!"

He turned back to Neverland and I made my way to the kitchen on autopilot.

What the hell had just happened in there? Why did I have to bring up Halloween costumes while Harry was watching *Peter Pan*? What if he were watching Donald Duck? Would he have said Daisy Duck?

But he wasn't watching his video of cartoon shorts. He was watching Wendy, and I was stuck with her. Sure, it was an easy enough costume to put together, but how exciting was a blue nightgown, matching hair ribbon and light brown wig? What kind of Halloween costume was that?

Before bed, I told Ken about Harry's idea for a costume. His face fell.

"I really don't want Harry to be Wendy for Halloween," he said.

"I don't either," I agreed. "I'll have to figure out what to do. I already told him he could be."

"What!" Ken's stare left no doubt that he was not happy with this new development.

"Well, he caught me off guard!" I said uneasily. "I just finished telling him he could be anyone he wanted."

Ken didn't tell me his reasons, but I figured they were similar to mine. I didn't want anybody making fun of Harry dressed up as a girl. There were no bullies on our block. But there were the two macho neighbor dads. I imagined them snickering as innocent little Harry climbed down our front steps with a plastic pumpkin pail in one tiny fist, Wendy's skirt in the other.

I wanted to protect myself, too. This wasn't San Francisco or New York City. If a boy wore a girl's Halloween costume in 1992, it meant he was going to be gay. And there were still the mainstream experts who espoused the theory that a boy was gay because his mother was domineering. I didn't really believe it. And I didn't want to care what my neighbors thought.

But I did care. "Domineering mother" meant bad mother. While I didn't want anyone labeling Harry or me, I had to consider the other variable in the equation: Being a controlling, overbearing, bad mother meant becoming *my* mother.

I had three days to reconcile myself to the idea of Harry as Wendy and be a good mother in the process, and I didn't want to screw it up.

So what was it about little Wendy Darling that made a floor-length blue nightgown so attractive to Harry? Was it their shared fascination with mermaids? Maybe her dress was the draw. I tried to imagine how my mother would handle it, and as usual, I decided that doing the opposite of what *she* would do was the best way to proceed.

In my mind, I could almost hear her say, "Absolutely not! No son of mine is going outside dressed as a girl. I don't care if it is Halloween. Playing with a doll in the bathtub is one thing, but a boy wearing a dress in public is asking for trouble!"

23

The night before the block party, I drove across town through a foggy drizzle on an eleventh-hour solo mission I dubbed "Operation Disney Store." I felt like a double agent—I was about to trick my own kid and shell out sixty bucks for a costume Harry would wear once.

Back home, I explained to Harry that the Disney Store didn't have a Wendy costume, but it did have a genuine Peter Pan outfit. I quickly took everything out of the package and held up a green, short-sleeved top with zigzag hem, matching leggings, and puckish brown, felt shoe covers. Then I flashed the showstopper hat.

"Look at this big orange feather!"

He reached for it.

"And check out this Peter Pan knife! Doesn't it look real? But it's only rubber, see?"

I stuck the blade into my open hand and Harry gasped as the rubber tip flexed harmlessly. He wanted that knife.

"Do you want to try on the whole costume?" I asked, trying to keep my hopes on the down low.

"Okay," he said, stabbing his new knife into an end table.

The next day, Harry refused to part with his fake weapon. I sighed with accomplishment and relief. Wendy was history! And I hadn't had to tell Harry that his parents didn't want him to go trick or treating dressed up as a girl.

Later, as Harry, Ken, and I walked outside at 7 o'clock to meet Harry's best buddies and their parents, we found Billy dressed as Count Dracula, while Allison wore a Batman costume.

"It's what she wanted," her mom whispered out of the side of her mouth.

The adults chuckled at how cute Allison looked as the Caped Crusader, but a sickening feeling passed through me. I ached with disappointment in myself, trapped by my own double standard. I felt like a bad mother, the wicked Disney queen who had lured Harry not with a poisoned apple but with an orange feather and a rubber knife.

In bed with Ken that night, I felt like crying.

"What's the matter? Too many Butterfingers?"

"No, it's not a stomachache. It's guilt. I'm a terrible mother."

"What are you talking about? You're a good mother."

"Well, I don't feel like one. I can't shake the image of Allison so happy as Batman, when I didn't let Harry be who he really wanted to be. This was his first Halloween, and I failed him. I thought and acted like my mother."

"You're being silly, Julie. Harry had a great time. Just forget about it."

"I can't. I feel like every decision I make is a big mistake. Like I'm doing everything wrong."

"You're making too big a deal out of this. Everything is fine. Just go to sleep."

Ken leaned over and planted a kiss on my lips that felt like a punctuation mark. He switched off the nightstand lamp and I turned onto my side. As my thoughts raced around my Halloween mistakes, I thought of a night five years earlier, when I was curled up in my childhood bed, at my mother's house, talking to my little sister.

June lay inches from me on the mattress in my old room. She and Jack had arrived in town a few days in advance of the surgery our mother was having in the morning to remove a metastasized melanoma. Both were staying with Ken and me, but my mother wanted the three of us sleeping at her house the night before her operation. She didn't trust us to wake up, drive to her house and get her to the hospital across town by 7 a.m.

I felt June turn onto her back. "Are you awake?" she asked.

"Yeah," I answered. "I can't sleep."

"Me neither. This is all happening so fast."

She was right. Only ten days had passed since learning our mother's death was imminent.

"Do you think you'll have kids now?" my sister asked. "After mother's gone, that is."

"I don't know. That hasn't crossed my mind. I just always figured I wouldn't."

"Me too," June confided. "I settled on that after mother's visit when Sandy was a puppy. I was training her on the leash in the backyard, when mother came out to tell me I was doing it 'all wrong.' I know that's what she'd say about my childrearing, too."

"Wasn't that the same trip she rearranged all of your living room knickknacks while you were at work?"

"The same," my sister replied.

I rolled onto my side and propped up my head with my hand. "Well, you don't even live here, June. Imagine what it would be like for me. She'd be over constantly, interfering, giving unsolicited advice. She'd want to babysit!"

I tensed at the idea and felt my shoulder scrunch up to my ear. I remembered the piercing looks my mother shot at me as a child. I flinched recalling the slap of her hand to my face. "How could I leave a baby with her? Who knows what she'd do?"

"Let's say we do decide to have kids after mother dies, and one of us has a girl," my sister said. "Does this mean we have to name her Jane?"

I flopped onto my back. "For God's sake, June. No, we do not!"

There was no such thing as subtle hints when it came to our mother's desire for grandchildren or her belief she could control our lives.

"I think you should get pregnant!" she had blurted in the bleachers at my brother's championship basketball game at the Jewish Community Center in 1979.

"What?! Get pregnant?" I'd replied. "Are you kidding? I'm not even married!"

"I don't care about that anymore. I want grandchildren."

I shook off the memory of the fears my sister and I had shared and snuggled up against Ken. I was forty-one years old. I thought I'd be able to handle anything by now. But I wasn't convinced I was ready, or that my neighborhood was ready. I drifted off to sleep telling myself, "I am not my mother, I am not my mother, I am not my mother."

Over the next months, as Christmas was approaching, I thought carefully about what I would say yes to and no to. Barbie had been a yes; Wendy a no. I wondered if dividing Harry's indoor and outdoor worlds was being too controlling. I wasn't sure what message I was sending him. Would he think playing with girl toys is okay, but dressing like a girl isn't? I didn't know what was right. I just knew I wanted him to stay happy and free from teasing.

The Friday night before Christmas, our twenty-five-year-old nephew Dirk arrived from London. Ken had been in bed for hours and I was moving around ornaments on the tree when the doorbell rang. Dirk was en route to his family's place in Minneapolis for the holidays and stopped as he usually did to spend a couple of days with us. He had just finished his masters in performing arts and was thinking of moving to Australia. He wasn't around much, and I wanted Harry to get to know him.

We caught up on our lives as Dirk tossed color-changing pinecones into the fireplace. The only other light in the living room came from the glow of multicolored bulbs on the ceiling-high Christmas tree. Added warmth came from a bottle of chardonnay.

"Harry wants the Barbie Dream House," I said. "And I'm so conflicted about it."

"I always wanted the Barbie Dream House, too," Dirk replied.

"Really?"

This was Dirk's first mention that Barbie had played a role in his early life. He'd come out to his parents in a letter the year before. I wasn't surprised to learn he was gay, but I'd never known he'd wanted the Barbie Dream House, too. I wondered if this were a sure sign Harry *would* be gay. Maybe Barbie was a genetic marker in Ken's family and a harbinger of Harry's development.

"I wanted one ever since I started playing Barbies with my sister," Dirk said. "I was seven or eight. A friend of ours had one, and we both wanted it."

"Same with Harry! Did you get it?"

"Not until we were about ten or eleven, when we bought it ourselves at a garage sale. It was stored with Andrea's toys, with the Barbie stuff. I was forced to be Ken. He always wanted a divorce, I seem to recall."

I laughed. "I could use a little comic relief on this topic."

"Okay, cue the wine, please," said Dirk, extending a glass from his spot on the rug.

I poured more for both of us and then recrossed my legs on the yellow leather ottoman. I told him about Harry's "inside my head" comment and my recent Peter Pan bait-and-switch.

"I didn't get him the Barbie House," I continued. "I looked at Toys R Us, but it costs a hundred dollars! The thing is made of the cheapest plastic ever and huge—three Barbie stories tall! I don't even know where we'd put it."

"Barbie dreams big. It's a townhouse."

"Yeah, well, there's no Barbie subdivision here," I said. "We're giving him a two-story wooden dollhouse instead. It's perfect for all the miniature Disney characters he has. But I still feel guilty; Santa is supposed to bring kids what they want."

"The fat man didn't get it for me either," Dirk said, "and I turned out to be quite brilliant, if you ask me."

"You are perfect, Dirk. Really, you are."

Dirk was a creative, theatrical, and fun. I could imagine Harry being like him. But Santa guilt was tearing me up inside, along with worry about keeping Harry protected in the world outside.

The day after Dirk left I got a phone call at the office from my friend Harry Gold, an architectural designer and artist in Los Angeles. His full name was Harry James Gold, and I'd named my Harry for him.

Days after my "you're-over-thirty-five" amniocentesis in 1989 revealed that Ken and I were having a boy, I learned from Harry

Gold that he'd tested positive for HIV. Ken and I hadn't even talked baby names yet, but I knew that night what name I wanted our son to have. I didn't care that Jews weren't supposed to name their children after someone living; I knew this friend I loved dearly wasn't long for this world.

When I told Ken, he thought I wanted to name our boy after his dad, a Harry who went by his middle name, Allyn. And, in part, I did want to honor him. I loved Ken's dad and was closer to him than my own father. The middle name James made sense to Ken, too, because his oldest brother Jimmy had been killed in a one-car accident when he was twenty-one. After I explained about Harry Gold, Ken agreed our son would be named for two treasured Harrys.

"Hey, Harry, what's up?" I asked, leaning back in the desk chair of my corner office. "You never call me at work."

"I'm having a party tomorrow night, and I want you to come."

"What? Are you kidding? Tomorrow night? Christmas is just three days away."

"Well, if you want to see me again, you'll be here."

The room felt suddenly cold. "What do you mean?"

"I've got brain lesions. My doctor says I only have a few days."

This was it. My beloved friend Harry had just uttered the words I'd dreaded for three years. And I realized this was the real reason I worried my little Harry might be gay. I was afraid of raising a son I would have to watch die. The thought of getting this call from my Harry some day caused a short circuit in my brain. I could barely process the information as a friend. My stomach twisted and I felt myself wanting to vomit.

"Oh no, Harry . . ." I heard my voice crack. "Fuck!"

I couldn't believe how fast it had come to this. We'd just met up for a long weekend over my business trip to New York six months earlier. Even though he was taking a ton of pills, he looked as strong and handsome as ever. But he had joked about his T-cell count not being high enough for a decent dinner party.

"Yeah," he said. "So I'm throwing a farewell party for myself. I'm calling everyone I know who isn't dead yet."

So many of Harry's friends had suffered prolonged, painful deaths, including his best friend Scott. On a visit to Harry the summer before, he'd handed me a book from the shelf in his office. It was called, *Final Exit: The Practicalities of Self-Deliverance and Assisted Suicide for the Dying*.

"*Final Exit?*" I said opening the cover. "I've never heard of this."

"It just came out."

As I paged through, my eyes jumped onto pairs words that held a sense of foreboding, like "plastic bag" and "lethal dose." I looked up and jiggled my head back and forth, as if I could empty my mind of such thoughts.

"Is this what you're going to do?" I asked, forcing myself to swallow.

"Not now, but I have to be prepared. I've started collecting heavy-dose barbiturates for when the time comes."

The nausea and dizziness I'd felt that day returned. Harry would be going through with his final exit plan and the reality of it pounded me with an avalanche of grief. This was too soon! I wanted my little Harry to really know his Uncle Harry. I flashed on the pictures I'd taken of them together in L.A. the year before. My toddler had taken his first steps at Uncle Harry's house.

"I won't miss your party," I said, wiping my cheeks with a tissue.

"Good. You can stay here."

"I love you, Harry."

"Me too. So get your skinny ass over here."

I hung up the receiver, my eyes still streaming. Then I got up to close my office door and burst into loud, uncontrollable sobs.

I arrived at Harry's house the following afternoon. People were already gathering. His sister Chloe had flown in that morning from Denver. She and I were the same age, as were our brothers. We'd all grown up across the street from each other. Their mom, Alessa, called me her second daughter.

Chloe told me Harry was extending the party another day so his friends in New York could get there. I was glad I'd planned to stay an extra day. Then, with eyes red from crying, she explained he'd lost his peripheral vision and was having trouble seeing anything that wasn't right in front of him.

When I found Harry, he was in the kitchen laughing, a full glass of scotch in his hand. He gave me a big hug, and I didn't want to let go.

"I should have asked you to marry me instead of Ken," I said into his ear.

"That's what all you girls say," he said.

I stayed in the background that night and the next. I'd had Harry all to myself in New York. It was time to share him with his family and friends. Like everyone there, I did my best to stay upbeat. But I could see from the whispers, the hugs, and the trembling drinks that everyone was on edge. Harry wanted a festive atmosphere, but it was hard to have fun knowing that the end of the party meant the end of his life.

I did a decent job of last-party denial until I passed Harry's shrine on an alcove wall in the dining room. It was a work of art, a tribute to his friends who had died of AIDS. I'd seen it the spring before: a large, hand-carved Mexican crucifix with names underneath in a block of type he'd written in pencil. I put the fingertips of both hands to my mouth and felt the burning sensation in my nasal cavity that signaled imminent tears. There were twice as many names as before.

On Christmas Eve morning I boarded an early morning flight home. I hadn't slept all night, knowing my closest male friend was drifting to death in the next room. I was glad I'd left the house before anyone else had awoken. I didn't think I could bear to see a hearse pull up and his body carried out. I couldn't wait to squeeze my little Harry and tell him how much I loved him.

I heard my son's small bare feet running on the hardwood floors as soon as I opened the back door.

"Momma!" he said, bounding into the kitchen.

"Hi, Peanut!"

I lifted him up and held his compact little body close to my chest. I pressed my cold cheek to the warmth and softness of his and whispered, "I love you." I breathed in the familiar scent of his skin and kissed his cheek. He pulled away and put his hands on my face.

"Why are you crying, Momma?"

"Only because I'm so happy to see you, Harry," I said brushing my face with one wrist. "These are called tears of joy."

He gave me a kiss on the lips and then wriggled to get down. "Come on, I want to show you something." He ran past Ken who'd followed him in.

"Are you okay?" Ken asked, putting his arm around me.

"I will be," I said, feeling my eyes well up again. "It's good to be home."

"We don't have to do this, you know. Jean and Marie don't have to come over."

"No, I need family tonight. Really, I do."

Harry was thrilled with the dollhouse from Santa, which we ended up calling the "character house." Somehow Santa had opened up Harry's storage bin of molded-plastic Disney characters and placed them all inside the house. Harry took the two red roof slats out immediately and placed Cinderella on the top crossbar, like the figurehead on a ship's bow. Tinkerbell, Wendy, and Jasmine got the master bedroom upstairs. Belle ended up downstairs with Mickey, Goofy, Tigger, and Pooh. I could only guess that her yellow, rather than blue, dress had held her back.

We also gave Harry the animated video *Robin Hood*, and it quickly replaced *Peter Pan* as his favorite cartoon movie. He and Heidi watched it most afternoons that winter of 1993. Even with all the characters as animals and Robin Hood a fox, I thought Robin was still a masculine role model for Harry and a good balance to Wendy and Cinderella Barbie.

The movie was playing late one afternoon when I returned home from work. I heard Heidi laughing over the music from the movie's ending as I walked through the kitchen to the living room to greet the two merrymakers.

I stopped in the archway entrance, where I did a double take. Harry was wrapped up in toilet paper, with a long, flowing piece tied around his head. He skipped around the living room in front of Robin Hood and Maid Marian's wedding scene finale.

"Hi, guys!" I said. "Harry, why are you dressed like a mummy?"

"Harry's a bride," Heidi said, laughing behind hands that covered her mouth. "He went into the bathroom and made his dress all by himself."

Little Harry looked adorable, and I knew his idea for a wedding dress was creative, but he was clearly relating to the movie's female vixen and not Robin, the fox. Heidi got up to leave and bent to kiss Harry goodbye.

"See you tomorrow, Maid Marian. Have fun with your mom and dad tonight."

Harry took hold of my hands and the two of us twirled around the room until I needed to get dinner started. On my way to the kitchen, I drifted into my own thoughts. I loved seeing Harry so happy, but he wanted to be a bride and this wasn't Halloween anymore.

After dinner, while Ken and Harry colored with markers at the glass table in the living room, I sneaked from kitchen clean up to the guest room upstairs. I pulled Dr. Spock's book off the shelf and turned to the page marked with the purple sticky tab. I read over the two paragraphs I almost had memorized. Again I was reminded that Harry might not lose interest in all things girl until the age of five or six.

Then, I put the book away and on my way back downstairs resigned myself to a long, long wait.

Striking a pose, 1994

The Dress-Up Box

We had a situation here today I thought you should know about before you come to pick up Harry," said Jodi, one of the bubbly preschool teachers at Milestones.

Harry had started at the year-round preschool and kindergarten near our house a few weeks before his nanny Heidi moved back to Germany. The school only called me at the office if Harry was sick. But today Jodi's tone was all business.

"Is Harry in some kind of trouble?" I asked.

"Well, after naptime, when the kids put their socks and shoes back on, Sara's tights were missing. We couldn't find them anywhere, and she became hysterical."

A small knot began forming in my stomach.

"We got her calmed down enough to go with everyone to the gym, and then searched the room again. Her tights were stuffed in the back of Harry's cubbyhole in the hallway."

"Did you ask him about it?"

"Yes, and he said he didn't know how they got there."

The knot in my stomach loosened. My little Harry wore lavender Minnie Mouse knee-highs, but what he really wanted was tights.

My car was getting a tune-up, so at the end of the day Ken picked me up at the marketing agency, which was just three blocks from his eponymous downtown design studio. We drove together to get Harry, and I told him about The Case of the Missing Tights.

"So what do you think we should do?" he asked.

"I don't know," I said. "Asking Harry why he stole Sara's tights doesn't really seem like the point."

"I think that's a good call, but we have to say something. He did take a friend's personal property without asking and made her very upset."

"Yes, that's it, Ken!"

I was happy to be married to a man who didn't think that hitting his child was the answer, and I sure wasn't going to be the mother who egged him on and then stood by watching it happen. I flashed on the single sheet of paper I kept under my desk pad at work. A national client whose CEO hired a leadership training firm had shared the basic principles of the program with me. As head of the agency's fast-growing public relations division, it became my go-to guide for managing people. Focusing on the issue and not the person was Principle Uno. Next on the list was maintaining the self-esteem and self-confidence of others. I knew Ken and I had to do both with Harry.

"We just focus on the situation and the bad behaviors," I continued, "not on Harry the kid who just wanted . . . Jesus . . . a pair of tights."

That night the three of us had a family meeting. And without ever mentioning tights, Harry understood that he could never, ever take something from someone without asking first. The next day, on my morning drive along the Lake Michigan shoreline, I continued to muddle over Harry's preoccupation with all things girl. More than anything, I wanted to understand him and do what was best for him.

For Christmas that year Harry asked Santa for a Mermaid Barbie. Not only was her blond hair the longest of any Barbie ever, but it changed to a rainbow of colors underwater. Santa delivered on Mermaid Barbie, because after surviving my Dream House guilt trip that's what Santa was going to do. No way was I going to keep Harry from experiencing Wendy's coveted visit to Mermaid Island with Peter Pan.

After a big family Christmas dinner, Ken's brother Larry, who'd driven down from Appleton with his wife Pam and daughters Vicki and Amanda, ages eleven and eight, spent the night at our house. The morning after Christmas, Harry and the girls opened Harry's new giant set of colored markers and were busy making art at the end of our dining room table that had been extended past the front door in the entryway to accommodate Ken's family and mine.

"Harry, what do you want to be when you grow up?" Vicki asked.

"A girl," he replied casually, without lifting his eyes from the sheet of paper he was coloring.

I stopped clearing breakfast dishes from the other end of the table. Harry's confidence in his answer made me want to hug him.

Ken, who was putting away CDs in the living room with his back to the trio of cousins, pivoted to me at the same time my niece Vicki turned her questioning face my way.

Oh, shit. Now what?

I raised both eyebrows and shoulders for the nonverbal combo that I hoped would signal, "You asked, he answered, and I don't know what to tell you."

"Okay . . . ," she said to Harry.

I looked at the little boy swinging his legs and happily coloring across the table from her. This was the first time he'd mentioned anything since his comment almost a year and a half before. Of course Harry would think he could grow up to be a girl. Ken and I had told him many times that he could be anything he wanted to be when he grew up. We wanted him to dream big and know that whatever he became, we wouldn't be disappointed. Ken's dad had hoped he'd be a salesman, like he was. My mother had wanted me to go to college for the sole purpose of finding a husband like she did so I could become a baby machine for her grandmother fantasy. We didn't want Harry to think his life was supposed to be about satisfying us.

Still, as I carried a stack of plates to the kitchen counter, I felt an overwhelming anxiety not knowing how this would play out. I was desperate to believe that the Wendy costume and tights situation were just Harry engaging in pretend play and nothing more. I wished it were that simple.

I opened the cupboard under the sink and reached for the sponge I'd marked "FLOOR" with a black Sharpie and wiped up a sticky spot of apple juice from under my foot. But what if that's what he really wanted? Then what would I do? As I rinsed off plates and loaded them into the dishwasher in order by size, I couldn't believe Christine Jorgensen was the only person I had as a role model for this. There was no one else I could look to. She'd gone to Europe for surgery in the fifties. I supposed grown-up Harry could just as easily become Harriet overseas. But grown-up Harry was two decades away. I realized I wasn't breathing and forced myself to inhale.

A couple of weeks later, still stuck on his answer to Vicki, I wanted to see if he was holding true to his future aspirations. When he rattled off that he wanted to be "a dentist, policeman, firefighter, or doctor," I smiled and wondered if he was learning about service professions in preschool.

"You'd be good at any of those jobs, Harry," I said, handing him a small bowl of fish crackers. Then I flipped on the TV to his favorite Nickelodeon show, *Rugrats*. Of course Harry doesn't know what he wants to be yet. How could he? He's three.

I had to stop freaking out over Harry's answers about what he wanted to be when he grows up. But what if he says "a girl" next time? I tried to imagine myself saying, "You'd be great at that, Harry." As I adjusted the window blinds to all slant at the same angle, I prayed I'd be able to come up with a reply that would make him feel good about himself.

For his fourth birthday in March, Harry wanted a Hot Wheels Race Track and some Power Rangers. He got both. His favorite Power Ranger was the pink one, but still, I thought the toys signaled a good balance. Maybe Spock was right. Maybe Harry would be in the majority of hetero males and I wouldn't have to worry about him fitting in with other boys or being picked on for his choice of clothes or toys. I felt some relief that maybe my tendency to want to control everything wasn't fueling any probability that I was creating a gay kid. And that meant Harry was going to be safe. He wouldn't ever have to plan a last party and kill himself at the end of it.

I felt that safety valve loosen in sunny open air a couple of times that summer. Ken's dad came to visit from Florida for a week. Gramps woke up from the nap Harry no longer took, and was surprised that Ken and I were home, but Harry wasn't. He wanted to take him for a walk to the playground at Lake Park.

"He's across the street at Allison's," I said, grabbing my camera. "Let's all go get him and we can head to the park from there."

I helped Gramps up the porch with no railing while Ken rang the doorbell. Then he put his hands on either side of his eyes to peer through the screen door.

"Gramps is here looking for Harry," Ken called.

"Be right down," Allison's mom Laurie yelled.

The bounce of little footsteps followed her voice down the stairs. She opened the screen door and Harry appeared from behind her legs. He walked outside wearing one of Allison's skirts, a pair of lace-trimmed white anklets, and a rumpled black velvet hat. The gold chain strap of a child's embroidered denim purse rested on his shoulder. Ken and I exchanged nervous glances.

"Now what's this?" Gramps asked with a flustered laugh.

"Harry likes to play dress-up," Laurie said cheerfully.

I looked at Allison clinging to her mom's knee. She was dressed in plain shorts and a t-shirt.

"Okay, Harry," said Ken. "Let's give Allison her stuff back. We're going to the park!"

I felt embarrassed in front of Gramps and was grateful he didn't say anything negative in front of Harry. He hadn't relished Barbie being in the picture I snapped of Harry and him the day before, and now his namesake grandson was across the street wearing his little girlfriend's clothes. But dress-up was just play. That's what I wanted to believe anyway. And I wanted Gramps to believe it, too.

My father-in-law was eighty-two. He'd raised his family of seven during the decades that homosexuality was considered a mental illness. I didn't want him to think I was allowing certain behaviors or mothering in a way that would predetermine Harry's sexuality. I put my guard up for the rest of the day, but Gramps never said a word about Harry dressed in Allison's clothes. Maybe he remembered Ken carrying around one of his mom's purses when he was little, and regretted scolding his wife in front of Ken for allowing it.

Harry would be ready for four-year-old kindergarten in September. After researching the local public schools, I learned they only offered half-day K4 and K5 programs. But we needed Harry to be in school full time. There were afternoons I had trouble making it to Milestones by the 6:15 p.m. pick up time. And Ken didn't get home until after seven most nights. Harry liked Milestones and had a lot of friends there who were staying for the combined K4-K5 class. Some parent friends said we'd have a better chance of getting Harry into the grade school we wanted if he attended kindergarten there. But neither Ken nor I could manage a part-time work schedule; he ran his own company, and I'd just been named president of the PR division I'd started ten years earlier. So Harry moved into Milestones' full-day kindergarten, and we didn't have to think about schools again for another two years.

Harry learned to write, kept a journal, and drew a weekly, personal news item with a caption for the kindergarten room's large display board. Most days I picked him up he was in the drama corner wearing a long skirt, flowered dress, or satin gown from the costume box. He wasn't the only boy playing dress-up, but he was clearly the one having the most fun. He made up characters, voices, and even jokes.

"Why did the lady trade in her black bra for a black-and-white bra?" he asked me one afternoon at kindergarten wearing a lemon yellow taffeta skirt covered in tulle.

"I don't know, why?"

"Because she wanted a zee-bra!"

I chuckled. Other kids still in the classroom giggled nearby.

"He's been telling that joke all afternoon," the head teacher Denise told me. "You know he's funny, right?"

"Oh, yes, I know," I said. "And so does he."

Ever since Harry premiered his Stinky Feet Variety Show in the living room, he looked for more ways to draw laughs. When a friend pretended her age was six and three-quarters, Harry piped in that he was six and four pennies. And recently he'd told Ken and me that when he grew up he wanted to be a scientist comedian who made rocket fuel out of chips and dip.

Before going home that afternoon I drove back downtown with Harry to the Boston Store in Grand Avenue Mall. I'd left work late and didn't have time to stop and pick up the black pantyhose I needed for a major new-business presentation the next morning. I told Harry to stay where I could see him and began thumbing through the Hanes control-top section. A minute later, Harry was nowhere in sight.

"Harry?"

I waited. Nothing.

"Harry?"

My heart thumped rapidly as I imagined him being dragged off by a kidnapper when he came running over to me, his eyes wide.

"Harry, where were you? I was worried when I couldn't see you."

"I was over there," he said, pointing one aisle over to the next department.

I leaned in the direction of his finger and stretched my neck to get a good look at the area. I saw a three-mirrored vanity table with a display of wigs on white Styrofoam heads.

I looked around to make sure the area was clear of shoppers.

"It's okay, if you promise to stay right there. And don't touch anything!"

He walked away. "Just call me if you need me," he said looking back over his shoulder.

Soon after, I felt a tug on my jacket. I looked down to see Harry wearing a short, layered gray wig.

"Grandma wants to go to the park today," he told me in a high, cracking voice.

I burst out laughing, and he ran off. I looked around, expecting to be chastised by a sales clerk for not keeping my four-year-old in check.

In a few minutes, there was a tap on my back.

"Excuse me, lady?"

I turned to see little Harry, this time in a brown collar-length wig topped by a teal blue bowler derby with netting.

"Can you please help me find the escalator?"

Again, I cracked up. Where did he come up with this stuff?

"Okay, Harry, put everything back exactly where it was. It's time to go."

A few weeks later Harry brought home a laminated smudged-pencil drawing of a stick-figure girl with a bow in her hair, titled "The Girl in the Fog." The caption, like the title, was in a teacher's handwriting: "Harry feels happy in his dress-up clothes." When I asked Harry about it, he told me the teacher had asked him when he was most happy at school. I imagined him spinning with delight in the drama corner at school while his dad and I sat in meetings at work. I wondered if the fog in his picture represented a safe cover for his fantasy or if it was where the real Harry came alive in his dream to be that girl. I looked down at his blameless face and gave him a big hug.

Later I showed the drawing to Ken and said I wanted Harry to have a dress-up box in his room. Ken looked at me with his head in a spaniel-puppy tilt.

"Isn't that just encouraging him to wear girl clothes? Are you sure you want to do that?"

"Yes, I'm sure. If the Marinos and the Smiths across the street have one, and the kindergarten classroom has one, and dress-up is what makes Harry the happiest at school, then he should have one at home, too."

The Dress-Up Box

Harry jumped up and down the night I put a cardboard box in his room filled with a pink-and-white-striped dress, patchwork peasant skirt, and short red silk nightgown I no longer wore. I also threw in my strappy satin wedding pumps, a few polka dot scarves that once belonged to my Great-Aunt Mitzie, a medallion necklace, and a white summer hat with a large black ribbon band.

He immediately put on the red nightgown, the satin heels, the hat and the jewelry. Then he ran to his toy box, dug out his lip balm necklace and wanted help slipping it over the hat.

"You look fantastic, Harry!" I said. "Go look in the mirror in our room."

"I hope you know what you're doing," Ken said, scratching his head.

"But Harry's so happy! And, really, this is just imaginative play," I said, not really sure at all if what I was doing was the right thing.

I'd gone back and forth about the decision. But seeing how Harry beamed wearing the tulle and sequined garments in the kindergarten's dress-up area made up my mind for me. I knew it meant I was now, more than ever, an active and conscious contributor to his preference for pretty and sparkly. I just couldn't deny him that same joy at home. At least here I knew no one would be laughing at him.

The dress-up box became Harry's favorite pastime. He and his babysitter Amy decorated it with stickers. Our housekeeper Angela donated some clothes her granddaughters had outgrown. And Harry squealed with excitement when I brought up a wig from the Halloween bin in the basement.

On a warm fall weekend, Ken's brother Larry and family arrived at our house for a family barbeque with the local clan. We were all in the backyard when Harry burst through the door wearing a skirt, t-shirt, wig, and heels. My face flushed, and I saw Ken's do the same. Larry was the first to break out laughing. The other relatives followed his lead.

Oh, no . . . is their laughter making fun of Harry?

Harry clomped down the wooden deck stairs and sashayed past us. "Am I terribly late for the party?" he asked, in a voice that sounded remarkably close to *Sunset Boulevard*'s Norma Desmond. Then he ran past us and back into the house. He returned with a different female get-up and drew more chuckles from his backyard audience.

"Nice wig, Harry!" Larry said, trying to control himself.

As I looked at Harry, smiling as wide as his face, bowing to his adoring fans, I couldn't bring myself to cheer along. Harry was still so young. He didn't know what cross-dressing was. Sure, it seemed funny to everyone now. But if he continued to prefer skirts and dresses, I was certain that beyond his own backyard the applause would turn into teasing and then quickly into bullying. I couldn't stand the idea of Harry being called a "sissy" or "fairy" or, even worse, getting shoved to the ground and kicked by older kids on the playground. But I had to be cautious about that, too. I was well aware of another mainstream theory that said an overprotective mother could turn her son into a "mama's boy." I loved my son who wore heels more than anything. I just didn't want him to be so different from other boys that he ended up feeling dejected, alienated, and alone.

Calm down, Julie. Bugs Bunny, Dustin Hoffman, and Dana Carvey all got big laughs wearing a dress. This is Harry, the star being born.

Then I remembered Harry's babysitter, the talented dancer. So who was I to balk at the idea of my son becoming a professional actor or comedian? Who wouldn't want that?

I unfurrowed my brow and clapped hard.

When Harry turned five and wanted to go to school in girl clothes, I had to do something. I came up with some house rules that weren't just about putting the right cap back on the corresponding colored marker or, after a crackled plastic Red Power Ranger, not using the microwave unsupervised. All costumes were to be worn inside. I thought that was a good balance between letting him be his happy, confident self and keeping him safe in the outside world. Still, I wasn't so sure and decided to call my cousin Elaine, a PhD in child psychology, for advice.

"Are there any men's clothes in his dress-up box?" she asked.

"Men's clothes? No."

"So put in some bright ties, a couple of old sport jackets from Ken's closet and some hats. See if he doesn't play with those clothes, too."

I thought it was a brilliant idea and added the items to Harry's dress-up box. Billy and Allison chose those clothes, but not Harry. I didn't understand why not.

As Harry passed me in the upstairs hallway wearing low heels, the pink-and-white dress and a light brown wig, I stopped him.

"So, Harry, let me ask you something. How come you never wear any of the boy clothes that are in the dress-up box?"

He scrunched his eyebrows as if to ask me if I were kidding.

"I already am a boy, so why would I want to dress up as one?"

Good answer, Harry.

"Well, okay then. Carry on."

And you're right, I am a stupid idiot.

As he walked back to his room, I couldn't help but think that maybe Harry knew more about who he was than I knew about who I was. And six months later he seemed to know a lot more about his cousin Tyler, too.

On a Saturday morning in November, a month before his cousin in Arizona would also turn five, I asked Harry what he thought Tyler might like for his birthday.

"Tyler's like me, Mom. He likes girl stuff."

"Oh . . . okay. Thanks."

It was true. Tyler had bonded with one of Harry's blond Barbie dolls during my sister's family's visit from Tucson a few months earlier. Tyler even took Barbie to bed with him each night. In return, he let Harry wear the black ballet slippers he'd packed for the trip. I winced remembering how an incident with the ballet slippers became the sequel to The Case of the Missing Tights when the shoes disappeared mysteriously the afternoon my sister was leaving for the airport. Luckily, June thought to search the bottom of Harry's toy box and the slippers were recovered.

The two boys had discovered their shared loves that weekend. Harry was right about that. So I decided Tyler's birthday present from us should be a Barbie of his own. I navigated through the Barbies, Power Rangers, and Beanie Babies minefield of Harry's room to the phone in the upstairs TV room. I figured I should check with my sister first. She was very particular about toys. I didn't know how a Barbie would fly with her. She answered on the first ring.

"Hey, June, I asked Harry if he had any ideas for Tyler's birthday, and he said—"

"Do *not* get him a Barbie, Julie," she said, cutting me off.

"Really? Because that's what I was thinking of sending."

"Greg would not appreciate it."

"Greg? Why not?" My brother-in-law hadn't impressed me on their stay that summer. Most of the time, he was either glued to a television tennis tournament or hiding behind the newspaper. Hearing he was anti-Barbie had just pushed him below the 100 mark on my hit parade of father figures.

"I didn't tell you this," June said, "but Greg was not happy that Tyler was taking ballet. He said it was too feminine of an activity and didn't want me to sign him up for any more lessons."

I took a deep breath and a seat on the couch. "That jerk."

"I wanted to follow Tyler's lead. He was into dance, but Greg was against that."

My sister proceeded to tell me how the disagreement prompted her to write to the advice columnist at the local newspaper.

"She didn't print the letter, but she sent a personal reply."

"What did it say?"

"She recommended we see a family therapist right away. Greg and I, that is. She sent the name of someone, and we went. It was horrible."

I felt my throat tighten. "Tell me."

"He was old school, very traditional. Bottom line, he said Tyler was into ballet, tap, and leotards because I was too domineering."

There it was, the dreaded word from a family therapist that described my mother, and perhaps her legacy for June and me, being amplified into my ear.

"What did you say?"

"I was furious he blamed me and told him I disagreed. But I had to compromise with Greg. So I said I wouldn't suggest dance classes anymore, but if Tyler asked I wouldn't say no."

I imagined confused, sad eyes on Tyler's face, but I felt more sorry for my sister. I didn't know what I'd do if Harry's interests caused a rift between Ken and me. I wasn't sure I'd be able to stay with a man who couldn't accept his child's spirit and imagination.

I flashed on a friend at work who'd told me recently her deer-hunting husband had insisted she take away all of their son's stuffed animals when he turned three. I just knew that her husband, like my sister's husband, didn't want their sons to be gay, like there was something wrong with it.

"June, do you think Harry and Tyler are going to be gay cousins?"

"I don't know," she said. "Maybe. You told me we have gay cousins on Dad's side of the family."

That was true. We had two second-cousin brothers who were gay.

"I'm inclined to think being gay is hereditary," she continued. "To think that it's the mother's fault is so ridiculous. As if it's even a fault!"

She was right, of course. Being gay wasn't a flaw. And I, too, felt fury. This wasn't just reading about mothers being the cause; a therapist had accused my sister of doing something wrong. Still, hearing the word "domineering" made panic flags wave in my brain. I couldn't wrap my head around why I continued to believe that Harry's behavior could be the result of my mothering when my sister was so sure hers wasn't. Perhaps it was our age difference. I was six years older, so maybe our mother's claws of control had relaxed their grip by the time she got to her youngest prey. I figured, too, that June hadn't been as exposed as I was to the cultural brainwashing that said a mother could damage her son's developing masculinity.

June felt no self-blame. There wasn't a doubt in her mind that the therapist was dead wrong. I wished I could just shake off the "domineering" label the way she did. I still worried I had unwittingly influenced Harry to develop certain behaviors. I wanted to ask my sister if she thought there might be the slightest chance we were enough alike to have set our sons' development along a similar path. Even though she wiped Tyler's face more than I did Harry's on their last visit and kept his nap schedule on Arizona time, I didn't think she'd ever describe herself as controlling. I had no desire to go down that road with her, so I kept my "what ifs" to myself and we said our goodbyes.

I scratched a pre-hives itch on the back of my neck and realized I couldn't share the questions with my sister that still swirled in my head. And I knew Ken didn't want to hear me talk about my fears or being worried about our son either. Ken was supportive of Harry, but I still felt alone as a parent. I twisted the curlicue of telephone cord around my finger. I just didn't know how to guide Harry. I wanted to figure out how to do right by him, because I had a feeling things were only going to get more complicated.

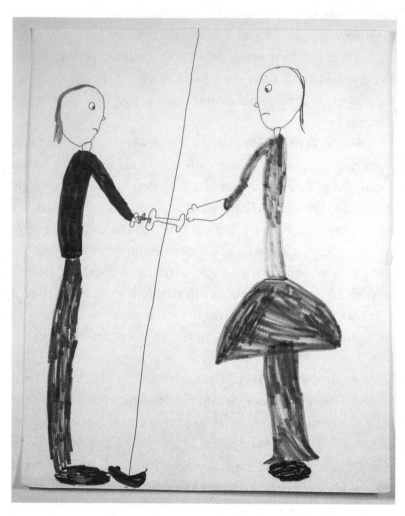

Harry's portrait of me, Mother's Day, 1997

Out of the Closet

I rounded the last two steps at the top of our second-floor landing, eager to get out of my work clothes, and froze. Bright red marks dotted the white built-in hallway drawers. Between the housekeeper and me, the white trim and walls in our house always looked sanitized, so this was definitely an aberration. It couldn't be blood. The first-aid supplies were on the lower shelf of the cupboard above, but I hadn't seen any Winnie the Pooh Band-Aids on Harry downstairs or on Allison before she went home.

I moved closer to touch one of the stains. I was relieved when the color smudged onto my finger; it would be easy enough to clean off. But after a ten-hour day at the office, I preferred not to spend one minute with a sponge. I only wanted to take off my bra, put my feet up, and soak in the peace that came with a spotless house. As I rubbed a dab of the smear between my thumb and forefinger, my mind jumped to the uncovered box of Clinique promotional-gift lipsticks stored in the bottom drawer. The evidence left only one suspect, and his name was Harry.

What was he doing in my surplus makeup supply? Annoyed as I was at the mess, I realized I'd never told him my lipsticks were off limits. Well, that was about to change. I leaned over the banister to call him upstairs, but then changed my mind and closed my mouth. I needed to think through what I would say. I thought about how my mother would have handled the situation and wanted to steer clear of her quick-to-anger responses.

I remembered running up our front steps the summer before third grade for a quick pee before meeting Janice Appelbaum at her house two doors down. Leaving the powder room, I spotted the orange glass candy dish on an end table in the living room, left over from my mother's mah jong game. I tiptoed over to the bowl and picked out a piece of hard butterscotch. I quietly unwrapped the yellow cellophane one tiny fold at a time, popped the sweet disk into my mouth, and shoved the crinkly paper into the pocket of my shorts. As I turned around for the door, I stopped short. My mother was opposite me, hands on her hips, eyes glaring. My tongue slid the candy into my cheek.

"What are you doing?" she asked.

"Nothing."

"What's in your mouth?"

"Nothing."

"You're a liar, Julie. I can smell the butterscotch from here."

My mother came toward me, grabbed my ear, and led me up the stairs to the big bathroom and shoved my head into the sink. She tightened her grip on a fist full of my bobbed hair, and I smelled soap. She was wetting the gold bar of Dial that sat in a grooved spot on the edge of the basin. I locked my mouth shut, but she forced the slippery bar between my lips. The soap scraped the edges my teeth. I gagged each time the bar of soap hit the back of my throat.

"Remember *that* next time you think about lying."

I hung over the sink sobbing and spitting as she closed the door behind her.

This story, and others like it, were why I was determined to create a safe environment where Harry would never have to lie, and certainly not because he feared my reaction over something so stupid. Resolved never to mirror my mother's method of house-detective entrapment questioning, I calibrated my tone from irritated to cheerful.

"Harry, honey, can you come up here for a minute, please?" I said into the stairwell. "I want to show you something."

He ran up the stairs and then slowed when he saw me standing in front of the drawers. My heart started to thump so loudly I was afraid Harry could hear it. I cleared my throat.

"Harry, I found these red marks on the drawers. I'm thinking maybe they're lipstick."

He scrunched his innocent face, and then nodded.

"Do you still have it?"

Again, he nodded.

"Show me."

I followed Harry into his room. He walked straight to his bottom bunk and lifted the pillow. There on his navy bottom sheet was a stripe-embossed silver tube of Clinique's Party Red lipstick.

I opened the tube and saw the mashed end of what had once been an unused stick. I imagined him and Allison standing in front of the mirror, gleeful. Party Red, indeed. Harry looked up at me, waiting, and I saw a trace of color around his Cupid's bow lips.

The thin plastic makeup kit with the clear cover his babysitter Amy had bought him at the Ben Franklin variety store was lacking lip color. His longing for a lipstick to complete the set was only natural, and he knew I had plenty of extra tubes. I couldn't be mad at him for wanting a lipstick. And I couldn't bring myself to scold him either. He was, after all, not afraid to tell me the truth. I wanted to keep it that way. And I wanted to feel good about reversing my mother's tendency to go overboard in the punishment department.

"You can keep this one," I said, handing over the tube.

His eyes widened to match his smile, as if he were seeing the lit candles on his birthday cake.

"But if it gets on your fingers, you have to wipe them off before you touch anything."

"Okay," he said, repeatedly clicking the tube cover on and off his very own lipstick.

"And Harry, promise me you won't go into any of my makeup stuff without asking."

"I promise," he said.

I turned to leave the room, but then stayed put. With Harry so happy I decided this was as good a time as any to talk about one of his school options for first grade, which would start in another two months.

When the principal and a number of teachers quit our neighborhood public school, Ken and I explored two other choices for

Harry: the secular private school that was a twenty-minute drive in the opposite direction of our offices or the suburban public school about a mile and a half from our home. The latter accepted students from outside its district on a paid-tuition basis.

On a recent tour at the private school, we learned from the admissions director that there was a dress code. Conservative styles aside, the only colors allowed for boys were navy, dark green, yellow, white, and khaki. I knew that combination of colors would add up to one big red flag for tie-dye Harry. While I didn't let him wear his dress-up clothes to school, I couldn't imagine taking away his colorful everyday shirts, shorts, and pants. Making him conform to a uniform of drab seemed cruel, but Ken thought I should float the idea past Harry.

"You never know. He might be okay with it," Ken said.

"I don't think so . . . but I guess I can give it a try."

I'd been avoiding the topic for a week. I knew how important color and comfort were to the boy who was now applying lipstick while holding the handle of a blue plastic mirror decorated with tiny seashells and glitter. But the school wanted our reply ASAP. There were other kids on a waiting list to get in.

"Harry, there's something I want to tell you."

"What?"

"At one of the new schools your dad and I visited, kids can only wear certain colors," I told him.

"You mean one day you wear all orange and one day you wear all purple?"

"Well, not exactly," I replied. "You can mix the colors you wear, but only a few colors. Just navy blue, dark green, tan, yellow, and white."

I didn't even get to the part about neckties and sport jackets starting in second grade before Harry's mouth fell open and his eyebrows crinkled toward each other. I might just as well have told him that all Barbie dolls were being recalled.

"Oh, Mom. I can't go to *that* school."

"We know," I said, biting my lower lip for having described such a fashion prison. "I just wanted you to know what some schools are like."

That night, Ken and I decided that paying tuition to Atwater Elementary in Shorewood was the only way to go. We wanted Harry to love school and agreed that first grade was too important to fuck up over some restrictive dress code. I felt good about the way things were working out. A lot of Harry's friends from kindergarten lived in Shorewood and would be going to Atwater, too.

I was glad to learn later from a neighbor that the Shorewood District's high school had one of the city's first gay-straight alliances. It was called SHARE: Students for Homosexual Awareness Respect and Equality. I didn't know an extracurricular like that existed, but I was impressed. Shorewood schools were not only reputable but also progressive. I'd heard too that the drama department at the high school was one of the best in the country. And then there was the odd coincidence that my mother had lived in Shorewood as a child. Harry never met my mother, but he thought it was cool he'd be attending the same school as his Grandma Jane.

When the first day of school arrived, I carried two large grocery bags filled with school supplies and the required two boxes of tissues, while Ken snapped photos. Harry was dressed in black bandana shorts, a signature tie-dye tee and black Teva sandals with purple and aqua trim. His new red, aqua, purple, and yellow color-blocked backpack rested on his shoulders.

I watched Harry navigate the throng of other students and parents all headed inside Atwater School. He waited for us to reach the four double entry doors at the top of the wide concrete steps before he slipped in. He knew exactly where he was going. At the suggestion of my friend Barbara, a grade school social worker, I'd taken Harry on a brief tour of Atwater the week before so he'd know exactly how to get to classroom 102.

I crossed the threshold into Mrs. Erland's first-grade class behind Harry and felt as if I'd been transported to the young children's educational floor at FAO Schwartz in New York. And if his teacher hadn't been a merchandiser at an upscale toy store, she easily could have been a set designer for Nickelodeon. Books stood open on display tables next to the stuffed toy version of their main character. I spotted a Linnea doll next to *Linnea in Monet's Garden*, the set Ken gave Harry two years earlier. There were Frog and Toad, Harry the Dirty Dog, and other familiar characters from Harry's library. Colorful banners hung above the chalkboards, while every bulletin board held an explosion of color. And all of the small desks were turned to the center of the room, so kids faced each other. Harry found his name on the front of a desk and slid into his seat. Ken took a picture, as Mrs. Erland welcomed her students and greeted us parents.

With her shiny blond pageboy cut, long skirt, print blouse and triangle neck scarf, she appeared to be a cross between *The Nutcracker* ballet's Mother Ginger and Mother Goose. I pictured her after playground recess on stilts, ushering the kids under a ginormous hoop skirt: "Come along, children, back to the class-room for story time." I guessed her to be about my age, mid-forties. One of the parents from Milestones kindergarten touched my arm and whispered, "Our oldest daughter was in this class, too. You are going to love her!"

After saying goodbye to Harry, I took one of the little yellow bags Mrs. Erland had set out for parents on a table next to the door. It was stapled at the top, and we weren't supposed to open it until we'd left the school.

I waited until Ken and I were in the car. And while he drove, I gingerly inspected the contents of our parting gift. Inside was a packet of Lipton's Soothing Moments herbal tea, a tissue, a cotton ball, and a folded note on yellow paper. It read:

Dear Parent(s):

Congratulations! Your child has made it to first grade! Having a child be in school for a full day can be an emotional time for a parent, too. I have made this little care package for you. After you have wiped any tears with the tissue, make yourself a nice warm cup of tea. Put your feet up and relax. Then hold the cotton ball in your hand. The softness will help you to recall the gentle spirit of your child. I will work with you this year to help your child grow and have a positive experience.

Sincerely,

Mrs. Erland

I wiped a salty mix of love and relief from my face. And I could see Ken was a little choked up, too. I knew in that instant that our little boy was going to be happy and safe at school with Mother

Ginger Goose. Ken dropped me off at home so I could get my car. I leaned over to give Ken a kiss.

"I had no idea I'd get this emotional," I confessed.

"Me neither," he said. "Our little Harry James is growing up so fast."

I clutched the care package cotton ball in my hand all the way to the office. I didn't put it back in the yellow bag I'd stashed in my briefcase until my assistant asked if I'd cut my hand. I felt like a sap, but I couldn't help it.

Harry's gentle spirit soared in first grade. He beamed every day that I picked him up from the Milestones after-school program that operated out of Atwater Elementary's cafetorium, the school's combo cafeteria and auditorium. He loved art class, reading, and math. And I learned that Mrs. Erland let him brush her hair, an activity Harry clearly enjoyed.

"Do you remember me telling Vicki I wanted to be a girl when I grew up?" he asked one day that fall.

"Yes," I said, looking up from my checkbook and a stack of household bills in front of me on the glass table in the living room.

"Well, I changed my mind. I'm happy being a boy."

I wanted to ask what prompted the reversal, but I didn't. "Okay, honey. Thanks for letting me know."

"And I think Charlie Brown and I have something in common."

"Really?" I asked. "What's that?"

"We both have a fondness for redheads."

He flashed his dimpled smile and then climbed the stairs to his room humming. I didn't know what to make of this news. I figured Harry was finding his way. And I was happy he was continuing to keep me updated with what was going on in his head. I knew his school-assigned "fourth-grade buddy" was the tall, auburn-haired Stephanie. And Harry had pointed out a redheaded girl with long braids named Jennifer to me one morning as one of his new friends. I wondered if this was what Dr. Spock meant by the "defining age" of six. Maybe Harry wouldn't grow up to be gay after all, and I wouldn't have to worry so much about protecting him from tough kids or bullies at school. I could just stress over him paying attention in class or not falling from the top of the jungle gym.

Over the next several months I watched Harry thrive as a first-grader. I was so grateful for our choice of public school. I couldn't imagine our creative son having to wear drab colors, plain white button-down shirts, and itchy pants every day.

Yet on a subzero February morning, one week after a snowstorm dumped more than a foot of powder across Wisconsin, Harry said he thought girls had "a real advantage."

"What do you mean?" I asked.

"They can wear whatever colors they want *and* play sports."

I felt a small dent to my heart. "Yeah, you're right," I replied, "It's not fair."

I couldn't help but empathize. Even though I'd let him take his pink chambray skirt to school a few months earlier, when he'd cast himself as Cruella DeVille in his own production of *101 Dalmatians* in the after-school program, I'd made the distinction that his girl clothes were only for play at home. I felt guilty talking about what was fair and what wasn't. The worry alarm sounded in my head; I wondered if good cop / bad cop translated to good mother / bad mother.

Downstairs in the kitchen, Harry packed his homework folder into his backpack and took a seat at the breakfast bar.

"How about cocoa and toast this morning?"

"Yeah!" he said.

I emptied a packet of Swiss Miss instant cocoa with mini marshmallows into Harry's Scooby-Doo mug and popped two slices of whole wheat bread into the toaster for dunking. I didn't offer Ken's favorite childhood breakfast too often because of the chocolate, but my mind kept backtracking to Harry's comment about girls being luckier than boys. I wanted his morning to have a little sweetness.

"Harry," I started, "I've been thinking about what you said upstairs about girls having an advantage, and I want you to know that things will be different when you're older."

"What do you mean?"

"Well, when you're a grown-up, you can wear whatever you want. In fact, there are a couple of guys I can think of who were actually famous for their clothes. Have you ever heard of Liberace?"

"No," he said, slurping up a bite of cocoa-drenched toast.

"Well, he was a celebrity from Milwaukee who played the piano and had his own TV show for a while. Your dad met him when he worked at The Edgewood Agency. He became famous not just for his music but for his clothes."

I described Liberace's rhinestone-covered outfits, his sequined jackets, pink-feathered capes, and big-jeweled rings. Harry's eyes lit up.

"You know that purple silk shirt of mine with the rhinestones and sequins that you wore for Halloween last year when you were

The Purple Thing? Well, that's probably what Liberace wore for pajamas."

Harry smiled. I knew he could relate. And I imagined him fantasizing how it would feel to be dressed in glittery glamour out in the world every day.

"And you know who Elvis Presley is, right?"

"Uh-huh," Harry said, wiping his mouth with his sleeve.

I ripped off a piece of paper towel from the roll under the sink and handed it to him over the counter between us.

"Well, he used to perform wearing a gold lamé suit—that's a shiny metallic fabric—that had diamonds on the lapels. And your dad probably has one of Jimi Hendrix's albums with a picture of him wearing a fringed coat and long silk scarf."

I felt better seeing Harry get excited about Elvis and Hendrix. But I knew he was more focused on how he felt and what he wanted right now. And that made me feel anxious. I wasn't sure how long I could keep up the dress-up box balancing act.

A few months later, the click of my black leather pumps along the high-gloss terrazzo floor at Atwater Elementary School echoed down the vacant hallway. I glanced at the Roman numerals on the watch Ken had given me for Christmas. It was four minutes before two o'clock. I would be right on time for the Mother's Day event Harry had been so excited about when I dropped him off in front of building that morning. He'd picked out a purple cotton turtleneck, black nylon flight pants, and his purple Gap sport coat. He finished the look with his multicolored floral necktie, and I noticed he wore matching purple socks. I knew the outfit was the equivalent of Harry formal wear.

"I'll see you later for tea," he said with a wave.

"You sure will!" I said.

Then he closed the door and ran off before I could get out my "I love you."

He hadn't had much to say lately about projects he was working on at school. "I can't tell you, but you're going to be so surprised," was his pat answer to any inquiries. Then about two weeks ago, wearing a billboard-sized smile, he handed me a pink invitation to his class's Mother's Day Tea in the school's big cafeterium.

"Wow, Harry," I said, opening the folded piece of paper. "This looks very special. What's going to happen there?"

"It's a secret," he replied.

I was proud of him for being able to keep everything so under wraps, because he used to think that a secret just meant something he had to whisper.

Halfway down the corridor, I stooped to turn the metal cross handle on a tiny water fountain mounted to the wall. I thought of Harry, just the right height to drink from this fountain. As I stood to adjust the purse strap that had fallen from my shoulder to my elbow, I imagined my mother as a child standing here, too. I felt a prickle of foreboding on my arms thinking about my mother on the day I was here to celebrate being Harry's mom. I used to dread Mother's Day when my mother was alive. Even shopping for a card was a torturous process of elimination.

Headers that read "I love you, Mom" or "For you Mom, with love" were nixed immediately, as was any inside copy that hinted at love or closeness shared. Those would have been outright lies. I usually defaulted to the funny card. A photo of a puppy wearing a flowery hat with the inscription, "Have the sweetest Mother's Day ever" was more my style. Even then I agonized over whether to write "love" at the bottom before my name.

I erased that memory as the soft notes of a flute floated from the doorway of the cafetorium that ran the full back width of the building. As I entered the bright room with its wall of floor-to-ceiling windows, I noticed that the space had been rearranged especially for Mrs. Erland's Mother's Day Tea. All of the lunch tables had been folded up and pushed back at the far end of the room and colorful quilted banners hung from the ceiling. The focal point of the room was two long rows of tan folding chairs that had been set up to face each other. The six-foot-wide aisle that ran between the two rows led to a tablecloth-covered refreshment table. The kids who weren't with their moms were standing near the cookie plate.

I waved to Harry's best friend Ian's mom, who was talking to Olivia's mom. I knew both of them from the preschool days at Milestones. My eyes searched for Harry, who ran over and hugged me around the waist as soon as he saw me. Then he handed me a handmade pink felt heart pin with "MOM" embroidered in yellow thread. I recognized the design from the Mother's Day Tea invitation. Mrs. Erland never ceased to amaze me. She'd given the kids a felt pin of her creation for each of the holidays: a black cat at Halloween, a candy cane at Christmas, and a shamrock for St. Patrick's Day.

I was wearing the gray skirt suit with mustard-colored vest I'd worn when Ken and I met Hillary Clinton at a reelection fund-raiser for Bill Clinton the previous fall; today I was the guest of honor. And instead of a metal Clinton-Gore button, I fastened a soft MOM pin to my lapel. Then Harry took my hand and led me down the aisle between the two rows of chairs, past moms chatting and sipping steaming tea from Styrofoam cups.

Two girls from the junior high who'd come to help their former teacher were in charge of the refreshment table. One was adding shortbread cookies to a flowered paper plate. The other turned the spigot that poured hot water from a large silver carafe. A third eighth-grade student, wearing the long black skirt and white blouse usually reserved for school orchestra concerts, was playing the flute.

After I picked up a cookie and a cup of tea, Harry directed me to the third chair in from the refreshment table. Resting on my chair was a large clay medallion necklace, glazed blue in the center. A leather cord ran through a hole at the top. I set my purse on the floor and put the necklace over my head.

"I made it," Harry said with pride.

"It's beautiful, Harry. Thank you!"

It was beautiful, but by weight it could have doubled as the doorstop for a bank vault.

Mrs. Erland asked us all to take our seats. Harry sat across from me and flashed a dimpled grin. His lively eyes telepathically broadcast the words, "Just you wait!" Beside each child's chair was a glossy floral-print paper bag that matched the plates and napkins. All the kids pulled out a decorative sheet of construction paper from their bag and took turns reading lines from a poem titled "Thank You to My Mom."

So many wonderful gifts emerged from that bag: a "Hats Off to Mom" booklet with pencil drawings by Harry of me as a teacher, nurse, cook, and more. Then came a thin hardcover journal filled cover-to-cover with Harry's colored pictures of us doing things together. In a large spiral-bound book of pink pages, titled "About Our Moms," each child illustrated one page about mother-child togetherness and another about an activity their mom enjoyed. They must have worked on these pieces all year, I thought.

Mrs. Erland then announced that each student would reveal a special poster-sized portrait of their mom as they read one last poem together. That cued the kids to reach underneath their chairs, bring out the folded portrait poster, open it and lay it face down on their laps. As Mrs. Erland said, "You may begin now," each child's face disappeared behind their artwork as they lifted up the portrait poster to face out to their mom at eye level.

But what Harry held up wasn't exactly a portrait of me. He was in it, too. I glanced left and then right to scan the portraits drawn by the other kids. Everyone else had drawn a head-and-shoulders portrait of their mom. Why was Harry's portrait, or double-portrait, so different?

One by one down the row, the kids read from the back of their portrait poster the line they'd been assigned from the poem. Harry's voice sounded the third verse: "It's a struggle to get through it, only mothers seem to do it . . ." But after he read his line, I didn't hear any of the others. I looked back at the full-figure portraits of Harry and me. I was standing in profile facing a full-length profile of Harry. He had drawn downturned mouth lines on both our faces. His expression was somber. I thought I looked distressed. Did Harry think of me that way? I noticed he'd drawn his pet hamster Hammy at his feet.

I wondered if maybe Harry had drawn full-figure portraits so he could elaborate on the clothes. His figure wore deep purple pants and a violet shirt. He'd put me in a short, flared pink skirt, pink leggings, and green long-sleeved top.

At the end of the reading, I clapped hard along with the rest of the moms. The kids stood to take a bow and then crossed the aisle to deliver their portraits. Mrs. Erland asked us to stay seated so that one of her helpers could take a picture of us with our child and portrait.

"Harry!" I said, taking hold of the poster. "I love this portrait. Thank you so much!"

I noticed a thin black line drawn between us down the center of the paper. His arm was outreached toward a circle on the line, as was my arm. For the life of me, I could not figure out what was going on in Harry's portrait. But I didn't want him to know that.

"I think it's so great that you drew the both of us together, Harry. Tell me about it."

"I'm in a closet, and you're helping me out," he explained, like it was just your average, everyday occurrence to be locked in a closet.

I instantly tuned out all other sound from the room.

What? What do you mean you're in a closet?

"Ohhh," I said.

I held my smile and felt my cheeks pop out like a chipmunk. I needed time to process.

"I'm so glad you think of me as helping you out, Harry," I said finally, rubbing the back of my fingers along the soft skin of his jawline. "And what a great picture of Hammy, too!"

Then before I could hug him, the helper-student asked to take our picture. Harry moved in front of me holding up our dual portrait and leaned against my knees. As soon as the camera clicked, I kissed Harry on the back of the neck and breathed in his warm, familiar scent of goodness. The kid was counting on me to help him out, and I felt lost. I had no idea what to do or where to begin.

When Mrs. Erland signaled it was time for the kids to return to the classroom, Harry helped me fold up my special portrait and put it in the flowered bag with my other Mother's Day gifts. With one last hug, and a thank you to Mother Ginger Goose, I headed back down the wide hallway with a group of other moms. While we all agreed it was a lovely event, I knew no one else's child had told them they were in a closet. I walked to the parking lot on auto-pilot, my mind flooded with questions.

My car had turned into an incubator while I'd been inside the school, so I opened all the windows and the sunroof. As soon as I turned onto Capitol Drive, my car phone rang. I lifted the handset from the base that was bolted under my dashboard on the passenger side and pulled the spiral cord toward my ear as I rolled up the windows. It was Jo, one of the account supervisors at the PR agency.

"Julie, I'm sorry to bother you, but are you coming back to the office?"

"I am. I just left Harry's school so I'll be there soon. Why, what's up?"

"Mark Campbell called. Carson Pirie Scott is going to merge with another regional department store group, and he wants us to come in as soon as possible to talk about the communications plan."

"Sure, but first I've got to tell you what just happened at Harry's Mother's Day party."

Jo was the mother of three boys, ranging in age from three to ten. I wanted a reality check on Harry's explanation of our portrait, and I trusted her opinion.

"He couldn't possibly know what 'in the closet' means, Julie. Do you think?"

"That's just it, Jo. I don't know."

She was probably right, but Harry had always seemed so wise and self-aware. He knew the word "optimistic" at three, taught me the word "oviparous" at four, and understood the idea of "abstract" at five. Now that he was seven, maybe he did know what "in the closet" meant, without really knowing.

As I drove back downtown along the lake, my fingers drummed a steady beat of inquiry on the tan leather steering wheel. Did Harry think I was helping him out like helping out with a school project, or literally helping him get out of a closet? I wanted to help him out, but I didn't know if I was supposed to help him out of something or help him find his way out. Then I felt a flash of panic. I didn't allow Harry to go outside in his dress-up clothes.

Shortly after he'd worn a wig, skirt, and heels to our backyard family barbeque, I had a talk with our regular babysitters. "You'll soon learn that Harry loves to wear dresses and skirts from his dress-up box," I said to each of them. "We're cool with that, but we don't want any neighborhood kids making fun of him. So please do *not* let him leave the house in a skirt." And even though I'd never presented it as a rule to Harry, I'd told him that the dress-up clothes needed to stay in the house. Now I was worried that I'd turned his home into one gigantic closet. I ran my fingers through my short hair and resisted the urge to pull on it. I was the one who needed help.

Inside the parking structure at work, I turned off the ignition and simultaneously tried to shut down my whirling mind. Instinctively

I took off my sunglasses, reapplied the lipstick I'd left on the Styrofoam cup, and reached for my purse. But instead, I picked up my Mother's Day bag and pulled out the spiralbound book I hadn't had a chance to look at yet. In it I found Harry's page.

In his illustration, Harry stood holding a paintbrush at an easel that pictured a heart with an arrow through it and "LOVE" painted inside. And there I was again, off to the side this time, smiling. I read the caption: "Good mothers give their children paints and brushes and canvas, but let them paint their own pictures." I paused, puzzled. Then worry gripped me again. Had Harry chosen that line?

I turned to another page and saw that Alyssa had illustrated the caption "My mother has the magic glue that sticks the broken pieces together." I decided the words were Mrs. Erland's and she'd assigned the illustrations. She knew Harry loved art. I stared at the caption again and knew that, intentional or not, the message was meant for me. I'm the one who needed to let Harry create his own pictures, his own world. That's what I had to do.

By the time summer vacation started, I'd done nothing about letting Harry's dress-up clothes leave the house. I was still mulling over how to let my son create his world when the universe decided one workday afternoon that Harry would be the one to help me out.

"I'm home!" I sang out, pulling the back screen door closed behind me on my way into the kitchen.

The heavy interior door, with its built-in milk box, was open so I knew Harry and Molly were home. Molly was our summer babysitter for the second year in a row. She'd been one of Harry's kindergarten teachers at Milestones, and he adored her. I felt like I'd won the lottery the previous June when I learned she was looking for summer work before going back to school in the fall for her teaching degree.

I hung my key ring on one of the white plastic hooks Ken had installed as Key Central on the back of the door. Then I clicked the garage door opener that sat on a shelf above the toaster next to a small vase filled with water and rooting spider-plant babies.

Just as I headed for the front of the house, Molly rounded the corner into the kitchen.

"Hi, Molly!" I said, half-expecting Harry to make an appearance behind her.

She hesitated. Her brown eyes signaled distress, and her broad toothpaste-ad smile was noticeably absent. I didn't hear Harry noises anywhere.

"Julie," she said, with a tone I recognized as "concerned teacher." "I know you don't want Harry going outside in his dress-up clothes, but while I was upstairs a minute ago I heard Harry go out the front door. He was wearing a skirt and a wig."

"Where is he now?" I asked, feeling under-control-mom composure drain from my face.

"Across the street with Billy and some boys I don't recognize."

"He is? I just drove up and didn't see any kids out there."

I dropped my briefcase and made a dash for the bay window in the living room. Billy wasn't a big kid, but some of his friends from basketball camp were taller than me. I hoped I wouldn't see the boy who'd made fun of the beautiful sunflower Harry painted in

75

the street at last year's block party. I knew he'd been inspired by Van Gogh and was so sad when he felt compelled to paint over it. I didn't know what I'd do if anyone was laughing at Harry.

Molly caught up with me by the time I spotted the boys through the glass.

"Will you look at that," I said under my breath.

Five boys were seated next to each other on the curb. Billy was on the left, then Joey from around the block, and next to him sat two boys I didn't know, one of whom was spinning a basketball between his knees. Last in the row was Harry, chatting it up with four boys who didn't look the least bit bothered by his outfit. He looked so damn cute I wondered if the two new boys thought Harry was actually a girl wearing her observant Jewish mother's wig.

"It looks like Harry's got things under control over there," I admitted, feeling a flush of embarrassment that I'd panicked in front of Molly.

"Why, yes, I'd say he does," said Molly, who was back to her confidently upbeat self.

Harry waved goodbye to her as she walked to her car. I heard her say "Your mom's home," but he stayed put. I resisted the urge to rap on the window. I remembered what Harry's regular neighborhood babysitter Amy told me the weekend before about the times she'd enforced our rule of keeping dress-up play in the house. There was no tantrum or crying, she'd told me, only hurt. Like it was something Harry just had to do. So now he had freed himself and was doing just fine on the curb with his skirt pulled over his knees. And I realized I needed to be okay with it, too.

I walked over to the roll-top desk in the entryway and set my purse down in its usual spot on the black bentwood chair next to our Lego telephone. I smiled, thinking Harry probably enjoyed giving those boys a dose of the unexpected. He still liked to perform, so anyone on the block who didn't know Harry the entertainer was possibly just another new audience. I exhaled an audible sigh of relief. I felt lighter, happier. Harry was outside dressed in girl clothes, and no one seemed to care.

I didn't say a word about Harry's outfit when he came inside, and neither did he. I asked if he had anything he wanted to tell me. He said he had fun painting rocks with Molly and then asked if he could have a Fruit Roll-Up.

I expected a dress-up-box parade from Harry over the coming weeks, but it never materialized. After his curbside chat with the boys, he lost interest in wearing those clothes outside. He still liked to answer the doorbell in a dress or skirt, and put on his purple and green Mad Hatter hat for trips to the grocery store, but the thrill of shocking the neighborhood appeared to be gone. I relaxed more and decided to chalk up the experience to a lesson learned in Harry's Summer School for Mom. Inside and outside the house, I watched my kid skip and sing and laugh. He was coloring his world exactly as he wanted to, with some shades and hues I'd never even thought of before.

Vampire geisha, Halloween, 1999

Not Like Other Boys

I was blinking a soft contact lens into position when Ken popped his head into the upstairs bathroom.

"I'm going to be out in the backyard with Harry," he said, gently tossing the hardball his dad had sent Harry from his early days as a pitcher on a Minnesota minor league team. "I want to practice a little throwing and catching with him."

Ken was usually at the studio Saturday mornings. Since we had Harry, he was the only one of us who still went to work on weekends. But today he'd taken the day off and wanted to spend time with Harry. I was excited they were going to have a morning together without me; something beyond our family bike rides or walks to the park.

"Okay," I said, dabbing my tear duct with a clean finger. "Have fun. And make sure he has his glasses on!"

I wanted to wish Ken good luck, too, but decided against it. Maybe it would be different this time. Harry, now eight years old, hadn't shown much interest in playing ball. His eye doctor had said it might not be as easy for him as other kids at first, because, with good vision only in one eye, he didn't have typical depth perception.

Ken had asked Amy, this summer's full-time babysitter, to do more sports-oriented activities with Harry. He did like the plastic whiffle ball set Ken had bought, she told me, but would lose interest after a few whacks. Harry preferred the bouncy dodge ball he used to play four square on the court the Marinos had painted in the street. But he opted for arts and crafts activities, imaginative play, and gymnastics over baseball or basketball.

I was putting on my workout clothes when I heard the back screen door slam shut. Then Harry's footsteps pounded up the stairs. Next came the bang of his bedroom door. Soon after, the slow sound of Ken's feet signaled he was on his way upstairs, too. He plopped down on the bed and ran a hand through his sandy hair. His mouth and eyes were both turned down.

"What happened?" I asked.

"Oh, jeez, I don't know," he said, shrugging his shoulders. "I was trying to give Harry some pointers on catching with a mitt when he threw it down and stormed off."

I softly closed the door to our room and then stood opposite Ken, leaning my back against his tall dresser. "You know Harry doesn't like to do things he's not good at right away."

"Well, I thought if he wasn't interested in sports maybe it was because I wasn't being a 'guy' enough dad."

"You do so many creative things with him that not every dad can do," I said. "Like those photograms of Barbie you made together in the darkroom."

He looked up encouraged.

"And, besides," I reminded him, "Harry wasn't interested in sports with Amy either."

"My dad didn't teach me how to play ball," he said. "He was a natural athlete and expected his kids would be, too. So as a teenager, I didn't know how to swing a bat correctly, and I got teased for it."

"You never told me that."

"Yeah, I excelled at creative expression, the things other boys considered feminine," Ken continued. "That stuff just came easier for me, like it does for Harry. But I got called 'fairy' and 'homo.' I didn't want that to happen to Harry."

I had no idea Ken had suffered at school. I'd always imagined him as the happy kid in the motorboat from his childhood photo album. There was comfort in knowing Ken and I shared some of the same fears and thoughts about not wanting Harry ridiculed. This was the first time in years, though, that we'd really talked about our feelings. Ken had seemed so distant. I felt hopeful this would help me open up about my worries

"It was the cool, accepted boys who hit the home runs," he continued. "So I thought if Harry had a little confidence, it would help him later on."

"If there's one thing Harry has, it's confidence!" I laughed. Then I heard a rustling in the hallway. I put a finger to my lips, and signaled to Ken that I thought Harry was outside the room. I tiptoed a few steps to the door, but didn't hear anything so I opened it. There on the floor was a small piece of paper. I recognized the shape from the notepad that sat with the small table and chairs in Harry's room. Just as I bent to pick it up, Harry darted out of his room, grabbed it off the wooden floor and ran back to his bedroom. Even though he didn't look at me, I could see his eyes were swollen. I knocked gently on his door before opening it. He was standing in the middle of his room.

"Go away," he said, ripping up the note.

"Harry, honey, what is it?" I asked walking toward him.

"Nothing. Never mind," he blurted.

"Let me, please, see your note," I said. "I love you, and I want to know what it says."

Reluctantly, he put the torn pieces in my hand. I reached to pet his head, but he turned away. I left him, closing the door behind me. I pieced the note together on top of Ken's dresser. My eyes welled up as I read his perfectly printed words in pencil:

> Dad I am not
> like other boys. I am going
> to stay away
> from you because
> you don't like me

I sniffled. "Come read this, Ken. It's addressed to you."

Ken took one look at Harry's note and stepped back, bewildered. "I don't know what to do. I just want to be part of his life."

"Go talk to him. Tell him that. Find something to do that would be fun for both of you."

While Ken was in Harry's room, I reread the words "not like other boys." Our sweet, artistic, funny boy knew he was different. I felt the urge to scoop him up, squeeze him, and tell him that everything would be okay.

When Ken and Harry emerged, they were on their way to Ken's workbench in the basement. With a huge grin on his face and a sketch in his hand, Harry informed me they were going to make "a big Barbie bed out of real wood."

"Come on, son," Ken said, with his hand on Harry's back. "Let's go. We've got work to do!"

I smiled watching the two of them head downstairs together. I thought the Barbie bed could be the just the right project to rebond their connection. Since starting first grade, I'd been the one who tucked Harry in at night, made his lunch every day, and picked him up from the after-school program. I had taken over so much of Harry's parenting that I didn't leave Ken much room. Maybe I worried that Ken wouldn't be as sensitive to Harry's needs as I was. When Harry was a baby, I used to be afraid Ken would set Harry on top of the car and drive off, forgetting he was up there, as he'd done with a cup of coffee more than once. While I probably had overcompensated to some extent, it didn't help that Ken often worked Saturdays and had frequent client dinners or deadlines that required late-night office hours.

I imagined them side by side in the workshop, finding the best piece of wood, drawing the shapes, using the saw and then going to the hardware store to pick out paint colors. I had a feeling they were going to find their way back to a happy place down there, and I felt good about that. Harry needed unconditional love. I'd thought Ken could provide that instinctively because his mother had loved him that way. I hadn't realized his dad's expectation for an athletic son was seeping into Ken's dynamic with Harry. He wanted to give him an edge at baseball to protect him from teasing, but so quickly shifted to what Harry needed more: a chance to be himself. I felt less alone in my parenting and relieved that Ken and I were on the same team.

I was still scared to let myself relax, especially when life had a way of sideswiping us. A few weeks later, we got the call that our good friend Jerry's father had died. Ken and I had gone to the funeral together that afternoon, but he had a meeting that night. So Harry and his sketchpad and markers came with me. He was happy to sit on the floor and draw while I mingled with people I hadn't seen in a while. I spotted Patrick, an architect friend who had an office near the agency. He was one of the most cynical and sarcastic people I knew, and I loved him for it. But I didn't see his partner Roger.

"His parents are in town staying with us," Patrick told me, rolling his eyes.

I was surprised, because I knew Roger hadn't come out yet to his family. "Really? How's that going?"

"Three words," Patrick said. "A living hell. We have to pretend we're just roommates. Roger moves all his clothes into the guest room, sets his parents up in there, as if it's his room, and then sleeps on the couch. I can't *wait* until they leave."

I felt sorry for both of them. Roger was a doll. I knew he wanted to tell his parents, but he was afraid they'd disown him.

"I sure hope Harry never has to face a situation like that."

"You think Harry's gay?"

"Well, I don't know. He could be. He certainly hasn't said anything to me. He's eight."

"I'd never guess he was gay," Patrick said. "But I wouldn't wish homosexuality on any child. It's a horrible life of rejection, shame, and humiliation."

My knees locked. "Tell me you don't mean that."

"But I do," he said.

Holy shit. No, what he was saying couldn't be true. Patrick had to be overreacting. I knew he'd married early in life because that's what was expected of an altar boy, but this was so extreme. We were two years from the start of a new millennium. I didn't want to believe gay people still felt this way. I wondered if it was because we lived in the Midwest. Would Patrick feel differently if we lived in New York or L.A.?

In bed that night, I didn't tell Ken what Patrick said. Even though Ken had shared his feelings so openly with me recently, I worried about letting my guard down with him. I'd felt shot down and dismissed before, as if my anxieties betrayed the makings of a hysterical woman. I just couldn't deal with that amid my worries about Harry in the future Patrick had projected. I rolled over in bed without kissing Ken, which had become the norm these days.

In my office the next day, I pulled my chair up to the Wang computer that sat on a side extension of my mahogany desk. We'd been connected to the World Wide Web for almost two years, and there was a website I kept hearing people talk about for ordering books. I typed in the address for Amazon.com. Then I typed "gay children" in the search box and waited. I sat up as several books appeared, but then started a slow slump after reading the descriptions.

Anything that mentioned "shame" for the parents, the "healing" needed for homosexuals, or included quotes from the Bible was nixed. I did jot down a few new terms I hadn't heard before, like "gender identity confusion" and "gender dysphoria." But none of the books addressed young children; the focus was on teenagers.

So I typed in a new search, this time for "parents of gay children." The same books popped up, along with a few more intended for parents whose teenagers had come out to them recently. None of those were going to be helpful. I felt discouraged as my fingers hovered over the keyboard. Then I decided to type in "gay kids early age."

This time the list of search results included a fairly new book titled, *Passages of Pride: Lesbian and Gay Youth Come of Age*. Gay youth didn't sound on target, but I recognized the author Kurt Chandler as a contributing editor for *Milwaukee Magazine*. According to Amazon, his book profiled six midwestern teenagers who'd realized at an early age that they were different. That was Harry! I put the book in my so-called shopping cart and proceeded to check out.

I hesitated at the box for shipping address. Where *do* I send it? I figured Ken would think I was just projecting unfounded fears onto Harry, so I typed in my work address. I wanted to read it privately. But then I wondered if privately didn't mean secretly, and I felt a sudden sadness. I was distancing myself from Ken again on the question of Harry's sexuality. But if I had to take this exploratory journey on my own, that's what I was going to do. I wasn't sure about typing my credit card information on the computer. It didn't seem safe, but I did it anyway. And I paid for overnight shipping. I needed that book.

When the package arrived, I opened it immediately and wished I could absorb its contents by just holding it up to my temple. But I had to wait to dive in, so I tucked it into the bottom drawer of my credenza. At noon, I walked across the street to pick up my usual lunch of a bag of popcorn and a bottle of cranberry juice and then closed the door to my fifth-floor office.

Passages of Pride was more than I'd hoped it would be. There were interviews with not only the kids but their mothers as well. My eyes watered reading more than one story of a mom who said she'd had ideas about her child's sexual orientation from an early age. Other moms had felt something about their young children, too! Not only had they figured it out on their own before their kids came out to them, but they had wondered what the future would bring for their child.

Harry was only eight. Even though he'd talked about a closet, the chances were slim that he actually knew what that meant. Still, I didn't ever want him to feel that he needed to hide. I wanted to be a good mom and a safe person for him to come out to if and when that day ever arrived. I didn't feel fully equipped yet, and I wasn't sure where to find the tools, but at least I wasn't alone.

I speed-read through the book over consecutive lunch hours, taking my time with the chapters I related to most. I felt an enormous sense of relief reading the sidebar chapter on understanding "The Roots of Homosexuality." It dispelled all of the widely held beliefs about parents somehow causing their kids to be gay. I remembered my fears the Halloween that Harry wanted to be Wendy and again two years later when he wanted to be the Pink Power Ranger. I'd redirected him on both occasions, afraid I'd be judged for a parenting style that had created a boy who wanted to be a girl. And if Harry did grow up to be gay, I knew some people would be sure to think my controlling personality and overprotective mothering was the cause. I wanted to make copies of this little chapter to carry in my purse as a handout for anyone whose judgmental stare implied I was making my kid "too feminine."

There was also a section about recent changes within the American Psychiatric Association, the American Medical Association, and the American Academy of Pediatrics to revise diagnoses and policies regarding sexual orientation. I was shocked to learn it had been only four years earlier that the AMA reversed its support of "aversion therapy." In another sidebar I became aware of an advocacy group called the Federation of Parents, Families and Friends of Lesbians and Gays (PFLAG).

There was so much I didn't know. I put down the book and turned again to my computer. I searched for PFLAG and learned they had chapters around the country. There was one in Milwaukee, but I felt let down when I read they worked with parents whose teenage kids had come out to them. That wasn't me. I didn't learn until more than a decade later how much they could have helped me.

Then I looked up "gender identity confusion" and "gender dysphoria." With one click I was directed to a page about a prominent child psychiatrist who still blamed a boy's identification with the opposite sex on an overprotective mother and absent father. I clenched my teeth. That's what my sister's quack family therapist had said.

I leaned back in my chair and swiveled to look out the window that faced Gimbel's and the Milwaukee River. No one would ever make me believe that a happy kid like Harry had any kind of a "disorder." Harry was just being Harry. And I had to make sure he could be himself without letting anyone get in the way. Myself included.

On my drive to work the following Thursday, I heard the radio news announcer break in with a special report. Horrific phrases hit like punches to my gut: gay student . . . brutally beaten . . . tied to a fence . . . left to die. I turned up the volume. I knew I was steering a car, but my arms suddenly felt numb. I'd never heard of Laramie, Wyoming. But now a gay boy lay in a coma on life support. How could this have happened? I blotted the outside of each eye with the heel of my hand. Who would do such a thing? Then I thought of Harry. I wanted to turn around, go back to Atwater, and take him to Fun World for the day. Instead I pulled myself together for work, checked my mascara, and sat like a zombie in a meeting about an upcoming new business pitch to Corning Ware. I could not stop thinking about the boy in Laramie.

That night, while Ken packed for a short trip to visit his dad, I rolled our living room TV stand close to the couch and flipped channels for more news about what had happened in Wyoming. I tucked my legs underneath me and kept the volume low. The boy's name was Matthew Shepard, and he'd been tied to that fence for over eighteen hours before a bike rider found him. I threw a crumpled tissue onto the floor and pulled out a fresh one. There was talk of a hate crime. Even though I'd barely touched my dinner, I felt sick to my stomach. I felt like I knew that boy and his parents. I'd sat in the same spot the previous August after Princess Diana's death, but this was far worse. This was a twenty-one-year-old college kid. This was someone's son.

My thoughts turned again to Harry, sleeping safely in his upper bunk, surrounded by stuffed animals. If he were gay, I didn't know how I'd ever be able to protect him from something as unimaginable as a hate crime. I decided I wanted him to go to the University of

Wisconsin–Milwaukee, a few blocks away, for college and live at home.

During the candlelight vigils for Matthew Shepard over the weekend, I felt the urge to step back from my job and be more present for my son. Ignorance about gay people had moved from discrimination to violence. And the two men arrested for savagely beating Matthew Shepard and leaving him for dead were his age.

Ken arrived home from Florida the Monday that Matthew Shepard died. I talked to him that night about taking a "radical sabbatical" from my job of nearly fifteen years to reinvent myself. I'd been thinking about a change recently anyway. I was running the city's top PR agency and had been able to travel internationally for clients. I'd done everything I wanted with my career there. I'd saved enough money to take off work for a year and figure out what I wanted to do next. I also thought it would be a good opportunity to spend more time with Harry. I knew he'd be too old for the after-school program next year. I picked January 31 as the last day I'd be pulling into a reserved parking spot.

When I shared the news with Ken, I couldn't quite read his face. I wasn't sure if he was happy for me, but he seemed somewhat supportive when he said, "Okay, if that's what you want." A few months later at the agency's holiday party, I was excited to kick back and enjoy my last big company bash.

"Tarney!" our IT whiz yelled.

It was hard to hear her over the band on stage.

"I just want to tell you how happy I am for you," she said, leaning in. "Congratulations!"

"Thanks, Carol!" I said, hugging her. "I'm pretty pumped."

"Yeah, well I hope Ken can come to grips with it for you eventually."

My mind did a double take. "What do you mean?"

"I told him how glad I was that you were taking time off and that you really deserved it. And he said, 'We all do' and then walked away."

"Huh!"

Was Ken jealous? I'd never considered that before. But why would he be? His design business was the city's hot new firm. He was doing great work and was even getting back into the darkroom again. I brushed off the comment and headed to the open bar for another dirty martini.

Those first few months of 1999 I became Harry's full-time personal manager and chauffeur. I got to chaperone a field trip for the first time with Harry's third-grade class. I drove him to and from summer art classes and swim lessons, with the stereo blasting. In the fall I volunteered to help organize the fourth grade's big family night event. And I picked up Harry every day after school, where he'd tell me why flamingos are pink or how his first-grade buddy wanted to be an artist like he was. I loved our car time.

Turning into our driveway one afternoon, a pop song playing on Harry's favorite radio station segued to a dramatic piano instrumental. A commercial advertised TV Channel 18's special report on runaways that week. I quickly shut off the engine.

"What's a runaway?" Harry asked.

Damn. Of course you caught that.

"It's what people call a child who runs away from home," I replied, reaching for my purse on the floor.

Harry's mouth fell open. "Why would anyone want to do *that*?"

I stopped moving. I wanted to put my hand over my heart, but decided to act unaffected. Harry didn't know it, but he had just crowned me Mother of the Year. He couldn't even imagine wanting to run away from home. By his age, I was already a repeat runaway. I was never gone overnight, because the Whitefish Bay Police knew my hiding places, but I remembered the urge to find safety from the name-calling and face slaps at home.

"Well, Harry, some kids have bad situations with their parents, where they don't feel safe."

"Huh," he said, popping the door handle.

I sat in the car for an extra couple of seconds. A warm mix of love and validation bubbled inside me. I didn't have to worry about being the kind of mother a child wanted to run away from. This was real confirmation that I was not like my mother. Harry loved me. I was doing something really right for my son, who counted on me to help him.

Harry was at a sleepover the Saturday night Ken wanted to have a talk out on the front porch. Sitting side by side on the yellow Adirondack loveseat, Ken turned to me and said, "We haven't been close for a while. I'm really not happy. I want to move out."

His words echoed in reverb. I didn't want to believe I'd heard him correctly. I felt my insides shrink and then expand back. As much as I was shocked, I wasn't really shocked. I knew I had distanced myself from Ken so much that we weren't connected anymore. I hadn't shared how I felt with him for a very long time. We were no longer lovers. We were no longer best friends. We were more like roommates. We coexisted. And that's not a marriage. He was the one with the courage to do something about it. I felt adrenaline rush to my head and down my shoulders. *How was I going to do this? Manage everything on my own after all this time? Wait, I can handle this. I'm a successful businesswoman. I can do anything. Ken and I don't need to live in the same house to co-parent. We just need to be cool for Harry.*

Ken and I agreed we wouldn't say a word to Harry until we had a plan. Then he got up to go for a ride in the 1990 Miata he'd bought recently. I watched the silver convertible back out the driveway with Lenny Kravitz blaring on the stereo. I sat still on the porch in the dark, while my mind went into crisis communications overdrive.

While Ken spent his free time looking for a flat close to the house, I put together a three-page damage control document that could have served as a case study for parents on how to minimize emotional trauma when you tell your kid you're splitting up. Harry was only nine, and he was going to be shocked. Ken and I never argued or yelled. We didn't get mad, and we didn't slam doors. Harry wouldn't understand the subtleties of coexisting in a disconnected marriage. That was too mature a subject to talk about with him. We needed to do this right so he wouldn't feel he was to blame, because it had nothing to do with him.

My social worker friend Barbara recommended a child therapist who specialized in children of divorcing parents to be our advocate for Harry. Ken and I met with her to write up key messages, anticipated questions with prepared answers, a timeline, and rules of engagement for us with regard to Harry. I covered everything. We were going to wait until after Halloween to tell him. There was no way I'd ruin his favorite holiday. He'd been planning his vampire geisha costume for months.

The waiting period for me was an emotional flipbook through events past, present, and future. One night before bed I looked at my reflection in the bathroom mirror and saw my eyes get glassy. I fought back tears that sometimes ended as fast as they'd begin. Maybe Ken felt alone, too. I wondered if maybe he wasn't just the braver of us. He'd had the guts to act on his unhappiness. But by the next day I was fuming about my upcoming status change to single mom who had just quit her job. My divorce lawyer said judges liked working moms.

I was still trying to figure out my next move when my former employer called. The agency partners wanted me to come back and head up new business development for the entire firm, not just PR. I did a high Tae-Bo front kick and then negotiated a sweet deal for myself at only ten hours a week. Things were picking up.

I stood in my workout clothes at the tall oak radiator cover in our front entryway separating letters and catalogs I'd scooped out of the mailbox. I shuffled past the utility bill and the postcard for gutter cleaning services to open a square envelope from the Waukesha Women's Center. It was an invitation to their anniversary fundraiser luncheon coming up in mid-October. The keynote speaker was going to be Gloria Steinem. "Yes!" I said, pumping a power-to-the-people fist close to my chest.

Gloria Steinem was my feminist hero and role model. I knew that stashed away in a file folder somewhere I still had the first issue of *Ms.* magazine I'd bought in college. And I remembered how extraordinary I thought she was when I learned she'd gone undercover as a Playboy bunny in the '60s to expose how women were treated in Hugh Hefner's club world of celebrity-like sex objects. I read her essay on that experience while I waitressed in college two nights a week at an upscale, bordello-styled restaurant. My so-called uniform was also sold in Halloween and fetish stores as the Naughty French Maid.

I recalled, too, getting an important All Points Bulletin from Gloria the spring Harry was five. I was organizing my jewelry box when the radio news reported a controversy over remarks she'd made in her commencement speech at Smith. Apparently some people were outraged when she said that women needed to raise their sons more like their daughters. They thought she was suggesting we raise our boys to be "girly sissies." But I knew what she meant that day. Her words gave me a shot of courage and hope that Harry's blend of masculine and feminine traits meant he was going to grow up a whole person. Those ideas were back in the news, because she'd repeated them in an essay about white supremacy crimes in the current issue of *Ms* magazine as a follow-up to the Columbine High School massacre in April.

I grabbed a pen to fill out the RSVP card. Then I noticed a box that said a limited number of tickets were available that included a post-lunch reception with Ms. Steinem. The additional fifty dollars for that ticket also included a photo op. I marked a big X in the box, wrote a check for the full-priced ticket, and sealed the reply envelope. I wasn't only going to see Gloria Steinem, I was going to meet her.

I felt enormous relief after reading Chandler's *Passages of Pride* and finding Harriet Lerner's *The Mother Dance: How Children Change Your Life*, too. I'd finally found comfort from outside sources, something I'd longed for, ever since the "I'm a girl" conversation with Harry seven years ago. But chapters in a book couldn't compare to a face-to-face with a cultural icon like Gloria Steinem.

I knew I'd only have a minute or two with her, but surely she'd have some silver-bullet secret answer she could share. I was desperate for a pat on the back and "You can do this!" and "By the way, try this!" Not having my own parents as guides, I found myself in search of someone to show me the way. All I had to do was figure out exactly how to sum up everything I wanted to know in one all-encompassing question.

The event was held in the spacious atrium of the Waukesha Women's Center's new building. I arrived early and waved hello to my friend Anne who was on the steering committee for the luncheon and a past board president. Her son David was Harry's age. I kissed her on the cheek and congratulated her on getting Gloria for the keynote. Then I asked which room was set up for the private reception.

I sat on the edge of my folding chair throughout the lunch and all of the speakers. My fork pushed around pieces of chicken divan on my plate. I was too excited to eat. After Gloria's speech and a round of applause, the executive director thanked her and wrapped up the event with a few announcements. I said goodbye to the women around me and pushed away from the table. Then I power-walked into the reception room in less time than it takes to say Equal Rights Amendment. I was the first guest in the room.

Gloria was talking to one of the Center's staff members. I lingered close by. As a photographer shot pictures of them, I strolled backwards to a display table of Gloria's books and purchased a second-edition copy of *Outrageous Acts and Everyday Rebellion*, which included several essays that had raised my consciousness in college. I put away my wallet and took out a black ballpoint, just in case Gloria didn't have anything to write with.

As other people entered the room, I made my way back over to the guest of honor and introduced myself. I offered my hand. She shook it, and I relaxed when no jolt of supercharged icon electricity blasted up my arm. Her grip was unremarkable, humble almost. She accepted my copy of her book along with the pen and opened it to the first page.

"There's something I've wanted to ask you ever since your commencement speech at Smith," I said, trying to speak without sounding like a 911 caller.

"Yes," she said, without looking up.

"I have a nine-year-old son who told his dad and me last year that he wasn't like other boys."

She glanced at me, simultaneously pushing up the bottom edge of her glasses with her pen hand.

"Those were his words," I told her. "I've tried to raise him without stereotyping, but I'm not sure how successful I've been."

I took a breath before my big question.

"How exactly does one *do* that?"

She finished writing my name and signing hers. She looked up at me and smiled. "It isn't easy."

What? That's it, Gloria? That's all you've got for me?

I pressed on. "No, it isn't easy, but . . ."

My voice trailed off as the photographer motioned for us to face the camera. I took my book from her, which was replaced immediately with the book of someone else eager to meet and greet Ms. Steinem. I let her keep the pen and stepped to the side, feeling like the girl who lingered too long in the reception line at a former boyfriend's wedding. I realized that my time with Gloria was over.

I stood dazed, searching for hidden meaning in those three words that played over in my head. I straightened up as Anne tapped me on the shoulder.

"There's Gloria," she said, nodding in the direction of my role model being photographed with someone new.

"I know. I talked to her."

"You did? That was fast!"

"Too fast, I'm afraid."

Then the photographer approached to snap a picture of Anne and me.

"I'm going to want copies of all these shots," I told her when she lowered the camera. I pulled out one of the personal business cards Ken had designed for me on my fortieth birthday. "There's one of me with Gloria in there, and I'd be happy to pay you for it."

I mingled with women I hadn't seen since the days I'd last had on a skirt suit and heels. Then I carried my newly signed book to the parking lot. It was time to pick up Harry from school.

I turned off the car stereo and gripped the steering wheel on my drive east along the freeway. Gloria's voice played on continuous loop in my head. I'd hoped for a simple answer, but "It isn't easy"? I already knew *that*! I needed profound wisdom or some feminist inspiration. "You're Gloria Steinem, for God's sake!" I said aloud to no one. Then I realized I was being ridiculous. She didn't know anything about my situation or me or Harry. She was probably barraged by thousands of people at receptions like this. I should have known better than to think I was going to get any kind of magic answer or support from her in two minutes while she signed my book.

After a snack pack of some Flamin' Hot Cheetos, Harry wanted to go play at Allison's. I changed into my sweats and went upstairs to the attic to check email on my blueberry iMac. I picked up the talking Executive Teddy Bear that sat on the top of the cabinet behind my desk. I'd had two of them, one for my home office and one at work. I left the one at the agency for my successor. Teddy always knew just what to say after a challenging day.

I smoothed his red felt tie and yanked the pull string straight out from the back of his navy-and-white pinstriped suit. *Pffffft.* "There's nothing you can't do!" Teddy told me. I pulled again. *Pffffft.* "You've got what it takes!" he assured me.

I wanted to believe Teddy. I had to trust that I really could handle whatever might come next being Harry's mom, and now a single mom, too.

Harry, age 10

Ken Hanson

Four Bullies Suspended

What's a hermaphrodite?" Harry asked.

"A hermaphrodite?" I repeated. I couldn't remember the last time I'd heard that term.

"Yeah," he said.

My eyes blinked in rapid fire as my mind rifled through words for the simplest possible answer. I checked the bottom of the indoor watering can for drips with my right hand, and then set it down on the black Parsons table in the dining room. Ten-year-old Harry was standing in the archway between the kitchen and dining room, opening the cap to a bottle of Strawberry-Kiwi Snapple with the front of his bright orange hooded sweatshirt.

"Well, I guess you could describe it as someone who's half-man, half-woman."

"Huh," Harry replied, with a slight nod. Then he turned the corner to the stairway.

I couldn't imagine where he'd heard the word "hermaphrodite." It better not be Ken's friend George again, I thought. Harry had come home from a recent weekend at his dad's condo to tell me he'd learned some new words for "vagina" from George. I'd expected "pussy," but when he said "penny slot" I'd been horrified. I'd never even heard that phrase. As soon as Harry was out of earshot I'd phoned Ken and yelled at him for allowing such a conversation to take place.

"Wait," I called to Harry. "Where did you hear that?"

"At school," he answered, bounding up the steps without looking back.

Now the "huh" was mine. I couldn't guess what kid was using the word "hermaphrodite" or where they had heard it. Maybe they'd come across it in a book. I remembered the oversized Webster's dictionary with the tan cloth cover that sat on a pedestal in my sixth-grade classroom. We took turns searching the tissue-paper-thin pages for swears like "bitch" or for words having anything to do with sex, like "masturbation."

I returned to the vase on the dining room table and picked a broken daisy from the freshly watered bouquet. I held the flower to my nose and suddenly felt a wave of worry crest in my gut. Had someone at school called Harry a hermaphrodite? It was hard to fathom, but not unimaginable. With his hair almost shoulder-length, people often mistook Harry for a girl. But having a stranger think you're a girl is different than a classmate taunting you with a word you don't understand.

On my climb upstairs to change for dinner at my aunt's, I reminded myself that Harry hadn't told me someone called him a hermaphrodite. And I wasn't going to ask him either. Still, I had an unsettled sense that something wasn't right. I stopped in front of the door with his life-sized self-portrait captioned "I LOVE HAMSTERS" and knocked softly.

"Harry? Can I come in?"

"Okay, Mom, but careful. The birds are out."

I cracked open the door just wide enough to frame my face at the outer eyebrows. Mango, the all-yellow female parakeet, was perched on Harry's right forefinger.

"Listen, Harry," I said, as turquoise-feathered Polo flew from behind the door to the windowsill across the room. "Rosh Hashanah starts tonight, and Aunt Margie's making an early dinner. We're not going to services with everyone, but you might want to change out of that Scooby-Doo t-shirt anyway."

"Okay, Mom."

"Thanks, honey." I hesitated before stepping back to close the door. "Everything good with you?"

"Yeah, why?"

"No reason."

After dropping Harry off at school Monday morning, I met up with Barbara who lived two blocks away for our weekly morning walk. Our standard round-trip hour took us from Lake Park to the Milwaukee Art Museum along the secluded bike path that ran parallel to the lakefront. Barbara was one of my best friends. She'd been a social worker in the Milwaukee Public School system for thirteen years before her husband's career took them to Connecticut. They'd been back a little over a year, and Barbara was still job searching.

"I need some advice about Harry," I said as we kept pace past the lighthouse in the park. "I have a suspicion he's getting teased at school."

"Ohhh boy," Barbara said, shaking her head. "Kids can be so mean. And this is the age for it."

"It is?"

"Yes! It happens all the time. Their bodies are changing, they're all trying to figure out who they are, and they can be terrible to each other."

"Well, Harry hasn't said anything to me specifically, but I want to know what to do if it happens." I told her about the hermaphrodite question.

"Listen, if some kid wants to make your kid feel bad, it means they don't feel good about themselves; they don't feel secure. It's their way of trying to have some power."

"Sounds like some adults I know."

"Exactly!" said Barbara. "But it's hard to explain that to a child who's hurting, to get them to identify with that kid."

I imagined Harry at recess hanging happily on the monkey bars, just wanting to play, and being attacked verbally with words that cut to his core. I shuddered. "So what do you do?"

"You can say you know it hurts and that he can talk about it. And he needs to know he doesn't have to let whatever kid it is make him feel bad."

I remembered the art project Harry had brought home from third grade. It was a large booklet he'd made of construction paper, called "Detecting Friends," with subheads and numbered fill-in-the-blank lines. One of the pages had been titled "If you're not sure someone is a friend, walk away." Harry had illustrated that reminder with four different-colored snakes.

"He knows to walk away," I said. "But he's still going to feel bad."

"That's why it helps if he can say something first that the other kid isn't expecting."

"Like what?"

"If he gets teased for wearing a certain jacket, he could smile and say, 'Oh, I like this jacket. I picked it out.' And *then* walk away."

"I like that," I said, feeling some hope for positive consequences. "It gives Harry some control."

"It really does," she replied. "He's being hurt by words, but it also has to do with finding ways to feel your own power."

"You're the best, Barb," I said, stopping to give her a hug.

Thinking of Harry feeling dejected, isolated, or hurt in any way was a trigger for tears. I wiped a thin bead of sweat from my hairline and took a swig from my water bottle instead. Barbara did the same, and we started off again. I felt better being armed with some tactics to help Harry. I hoped they were an insurance policy I'd never need.

Harry was quiet in the car on the way home from school that afternoon.

"Anything you want to talk about?" I asked.

"No," he replied, fidgeting with the miniature toy stuffed gorilla that came attached to his Kipling backpack.

Something wasn't right. Harry was usually more talkative.

At home, he dropped his backpack on the storage seat in the kitchen and walked past the fridge. I followed him into the living room where he sat on the radiator cover bench staring out the front window.

"Don't you want a snack?" I asked.

"Not right now," he replied.

I sat down beside him. "You seem kinda down, honey. Did something happen at school today?"

He turned his gaze toward me. His eyes had the same look they did the day we had to leave a dying Hammy at the vet's office.

"Jason's been calling me names on the playground," he said softly.

I felt every hair on my arms stand up like magnetized metal shavings. "Jason?! I thought he was your friend."

Harry had become friendly with Jason at school the year before. They'd formed the Nerd Squad foursquare team together at recess. He'd come over to help Harry screen-print t-shirts for the team in our basement. And he was at Harry's birthday party at the pottery shop in March.

"Not anymore," Harry said. "There are some mean boys in our class. He hangs out with them."

"What did he call you?"

"Just some names. It doesn't matter."

"It does matter if your feelings are hurt. And I can tell that you're hurting right now."

Harry looked up, but didn't say anything.

"Sweetheart," I said, gently rubbing his arm. "You know you can tell me anything."

Harry's eyes searched mine. "He calls me a girl. In the hallways, he'll walk past me and say, 'Hey, what are you, a girl?' I try to ignore him, but it's hard."

Fuck! I felt my heart rate accelerate as I brushed a hair away from Harry's glasses. I imagined the other names Jason called him. Faggot. Fairy. The same hateful slurs Ken had been subjected to in high school. But this was fifth grade! I wanted to pick up the phone and call Jason's mother.

"The other mean boys call me names on the playground, too."

I fought rage while Harry held back tears.

"Oh, honey, I'm sorry this is happening. No one deserves to be teased or picked on. Did you tell the playground supervisor?"

"No."

"Well, I have a good mind to call the principal."

"No!" Harry said, sitting up straight. "That would only make things worse."

I understood his fear of potential backlash for "telling." But I felt helpless doing nothing. I wished I had a magic wand that could solve everything instantly.

"Okay, I won't say anything." I promised. "But, you know, I think Jason has some serious problems. My guess is he doesn't like himself very much. Kids who put other kids down do it because it's the only way they know how to feel good about themselves."

Harry scrunched his face

"I know it's messed up, but he's probably not a very happy kid."

Barbara was right. It was hard trying to get Harry to think about the bully when he was feeling so wounded.

"Let's play a game!" I said. "We'll call it the Payback Game."

Harry perked up. "What's that?"

"It's an imagination game, like in your improv class. Think about what you could do—without pushing him off the top of the monkey bars, that is—that would get back at him."

Harry scratched his head. Then I saw the corners of his mouth turn up. "I could write Jason's name in some Barney underwear and then leave it in the middle of the hallway."

I smiled. Harry hated that singing purple dinosaur Barney. "The kid actors on *Barney* must do it for the money," he'd said recently flipping through channels on the TV. "I can't think of any other reason, unless it's for free diapers." I got a kick out of knowing Harry's creativity also flourished in times that called for revenge.

"That is so funny, Harry! Can't you just picture Jason's face when he found out?"

We both laughed. And it felt good to see Harry back to happy.

The Smiths' van pulled up in front of their house and Harry turned his attention to Allison, Cindy, and the twins piling out of the back seat.

"I think I'll go over across the street for a while."

"Sure, honey, but first I want to give you a hug."

He put his arms around my neck. I held him to my heart and breathed in his coconut-scented hair conditioner, not wanting to let go. He pulled away as he stood up and then ran out the front door. Thank heaven for the Smiths, I thought, watching the twins jump on Harry. I wanted him to get his joy back at school, too.

Back in the kitchen, I started to cut up a clove of garlic with the portable phone tucked between my ear and my shoulder. I was relieved when Barbara answered and quickly filled her in on my conversation with Harry.

"I'm still tempted to call the principal and ask him to expel Jason and his little gang of hate," I said.

"See how it goes this week," she said. "If the situation doesn't improve, think about calling his teacher. That's how it usually works. Then the teacher brings in the principal if he or she thinks it's necessary."

"Barbara, I have no faith whatsoever in Harry's teacher to effectively manage anything."

Ken and I had both been at Atwater's teacher orientation a few weeks earlier. In the hallway afterwards I'd agreed when Ken said Mr. Lynn was not the brightest bulb on the tree.

"And, besides," I added, "I want to honor Harry's request not to call anyone, hard as that is."

"I know," she said. "But remember, Harry doesn't just have to walk away. He can come back with something that's not hurtful. He can say, 'I like how I look.'"

"Thanks, Barb. I'll keep you posted."

Two days after our talk, Harry didn't want to get up for school. He still wasn't out of bed after several wake-up nudges from the door. So I opened the lid on the red and yellow maze of plastic tubes that was Chewy's cage and scooped him out of a corner mound of fluff and cedar shavings. His nose sniffed my thumb as I climbed the ladder to Harry's top bunk single-handedly. Then I put Chewy on top of Harry's head. It was the surest way I knew to get him up in a good mood.

"I don't want to go to school," Harry groaned, reaching for his pet and rolling up on one elbow.

"Do you feel sick, honey?" I touched the back of my hand to his forehead.

He lay back, letting Chewy crawl across the top of his nightshirt. "No, I just don't feel like going."

I felt the monster that was my anxiety rousing. This wasn't like Harry. He was a slow riser, but once awake he was typically eager for the school day. His attendance was nearly perfect. I just knew he was dreading the prospect of another day as the target of Jason and the other ten-year-old delinquents. I gripped the ladder with both hands. I wanted to let him stay home feeling safe, but I didn't want to set a precedent for missing school "just because."

"Harry, unless you have a fever or are throwing up, I really have to go into the office today."

"Oookaaay," he said. "I'll be right down."

I hadn't anticipated Harry not wanting to go to school. I decided sending him to school was the right thing to do. If I didn't there was the chance he'd want to stay home the next day, too. Then the guilt ghost sidled up, alongside my anxiety. It haunted me on the drive to work and followed me from the parking lot to my desk.

How could I truly protect Harry from a next round of hurtful insults? I wondered if he was going to be okay at recess and lunchtime. I wanted the playground supervisor to be my hired PI. Maybe I should have insisted on phoning the principal or, at the very least, Jason's mother. I liked her. We'd met when Jason and Harry were in Cub Scouts together in second grade. But I had to keep my word to Harry and not contact anyone. Instead, I opened the folder of prospective client companies I really did need to call. I adjusted my phone headset and dialed the number for my contact at Kraft Foods in Illinois.

I arrived at school that afternoon before the bell rang and parked in my usual pick-up spot on the Maryland Avenue side of Atwater Elementary. A mom with a preschooler was slipping her child into one of the baby seats on the swing set in front of the kindergarten building. I sighed with hope that Harry's day had been as easy as reaching for the sky on the swings.

When I heard the school bell ring, I leaned onto the armrest between the seats to get a better view out the passenger window of kids leaving the school. I waved to Harry, then sat up and started the engine.

"Hi, Mom," he said, opening the door. He dropped his backpack on the floor, climbed in, and fastened his seat belt.

"Hi, honey. How was your day?"

"Fine," he said.

"No problems?"

"Nope."

Thank God! "Oh, Harry, I'm so glad to hear that!"

He didn't seem to hear me. He was waving at his classmates Grace and Kayla as they crossed the street at the stoplight in front of us. I turned right for our drive across town to see the orthodontist. Harry turned up the volume on the radio to sing along with Christina Aguilera's "Come On Over Baby." A few more days like this and I could stop worrying about whether or not Harry was safe at school.

I had a new-business meeting out of town the following day with a prospective client for the agency. I didn't want to worry about getting back in time to pick up Harry, so I asked Allison's mom if Harry could hitch a ride home with them. I told Harry where Laurie parked and said I'd leave the back door unlocked with the alarm on. All he had to do was press the code on the keypad.

I was already home when I heard Harry enter the kitchen. I looked at my watch. I thought it odd that Harry hadn't wanted to stay at the Smiths' for a while after school. Maybe Allison had soccer practice. His backpack hit the window seat with a thud, and he brushed past me as a fast blur of orange without looking up or saying hello.

"Harry, wait!" I said, but he was already running up the stairs.

His bedroom door thundered shut. I bolted up after him, my heart pounding. This was not good. I knocked once and simultaneously opened the door. Harry stood at the double windows that faced the street. A multicolored yarn dreamcatcher he'd made at day camp dangled above him. His head was down.

"Harry, what is it?" I asked, walking over to him. He was holding the pin-art toy, making an impression of his other hand by pushing it into the framed pinheads.

"Look at me, honey."

He turned. His lower lip quivered and a single tear rolled down his cheek.

Oh, my God. My happy-go-lucky kid, wearing a Peace Bug t-shirt and happy-face beaded necklace, was silently crying.

"What happened, Harry?" I asked, kneeling at his side. "Was it Jason?"

Harry didn't answer.

"Please, Harry, tell me what's gotten you so upset. I have to know."

"He and the other boys were calling me names on the playground after lunch. I ignored them and walked away, but they didn't stop."

He sniffled. I grabbed a tissue from the box in his top bunk and returned to his side.

"And afterwards, in class, they ... were ..."

His voice trailed off.

"It's okay, Harry," I said. I took the pin-box toy out of his hand and gently pulled him closer. "Take your time. They were what?"

His eyebrows lifted and reached for each other. It was the same expression I'd seen in June after he'd reluctantly climbed into a scary midway ride with Ian at Summerfest. I hated myself for making him relive the day, but I had to know.

"They were . . . sticking me in the back . . . with sharp pencils. It hurt . . . a lot."

"Oh, my God, Harry! Sticking you with pencils?! Let me see."

Harry lifted up his shirt. I touched his back, looking for marks. When I was sure that nothing had pierced the skin, I turned him around and pulled him into a mother-bear hug. He burst into tears, and his small sobs tore at the corners of my heart. As I held him, petting his head, my eyes started to burn. This was beyond cruel teasing; this was assault.

I set my jaw and vowed to protect him the way I wished my mother had protected me.

I was suddenly back in my childhood home in Whitefish Bay, the same age as Harry, hunched in a ball under the blanket on my bed. I had trembled at the sound of my father's shoes pounding up the stairs. I knew he was coming for me, just as my mother had promised me he would.

My mother's nostrils flared. "You're the one who trampled the Polinskis' flower beds? What on earth is wrong with you?"

"But, Mom, it wasn't me!" My knees bounced with each word. "I only said I did it because Tommy Polinski was ripping the heads off grasshoppers and throwing them at me! I knew that would make him stop."

"I know when you're lying, Julie. Go to your room and wait until your father gets home. You're really going to get it this time."

The door to my bedroom swung open and banged the wall. I tucked my head and tightened the covers around my eyes. When I heard the clink of my father's belt buckle followed by the fast slide of leather through the loops, I stopped breathing. He pulled off the shield of my bedspread and began whipping me on the back.

"Destroying things? Lying?"

"No, no, I didn't do it! I love you, Daddy! I love you! I love you!"

I flailed around the bed, trying to escape the next lash. I saw my mother leaning against the doorway with her arms crossed, watching.

"Okay, Don. That's enough," my mother said finally, as if calling off an attack dog.

No one was going to stab my son in the back and get away with it. My scalp prickled and I felt my ears grow hot. After a minute, Harry calmed down. With a red, tear-streaked face, he asked for another Kleenex and blew his nose. I could no longer stand by. Something had to be done. I chose my next words carefully.

"Harry, this is no longer teasing. It's harassment."

I knew he'd learned that word in periodic classroom sessions with Mrs. Needham, the school guidance counselor. He took a deep breath that signaled he understood the seriousness of the situation.

"I want you to know that I must call the principal."

He nodded.

"I need to know the names of the other boys and what they called you on the playground."

I wrote down the names of the guilty on a small piece of note-paper from the pad on Harry's desk, but he hesitated telling me what words they'd used to torment him.

"Harry, please, this is important."

"Needle dick."

For God's sake.

"What else?"

"Hermaphrodite."

"Anything else?"

"Faggot."

Those fucking little brats!

"Thank you for telling me, Harry," I said, resting a hand on his shoulder. "And let me tell you something. I promise you those boys are never going to bother you again."

I closed his bedroom door behind me. My head was throbbing. I'd made a big promise in there. I looked at my watch. It was four o'clock; the Atwater office was still open. I'd never spoken with Dr. Stewart. He was hired from the public Montessori school when Harry was in second grade. I had no idea how he was going to react or respond.

I paced the perimeter of our entire first floor. Would he try to blame Harry? Saying he'd brought this on himself somehow? Would he say I should have called the boys' parents instead of the school? I picked up the portable phone in the kitchen and paged through the Atwater Directory for the principal's direct line. I dialed the number and took a seat at the breakfast bar. Dr. Stewart's secretary said he was available and transferred me right through to him.

"Hello, Dr. Stewart. This is Julie Tarney. My son Harry is in Mr. Lynn's class. Something happened in the classroom today that has me extremely concerned."

I told him everything that had happened that week. "Name calling on the playground is one thing," I said. "But being stabbed multiple times in the back with sharp pencils is assault. In my mind it borders on a hate crime."

There was a long, uncomfortable silence. While I waited for him to speak, I felt my eyes water. I wondered if Matthew Shepard's mother had ever needed to call the principal at her son's middle school.

"I don't want you to worry, Ms. Tarney," the principal said finally. "It's our job to protect your son. I'll take care of it. And I'll get back to you."

I inhaled five short emotional breaths through my nose.

"Thank you, Dr. Stewart. You have no idea how relieved I am to hear you say that."

I set down the phone and immediately clasped both hands tightly over my mouth. I squeezed my eyes shut and bent over at the waist. I wailed loud muffled sounds into my palm. This was the kind of relief Harry didn't need to hear. I opened the cupboard above the kitchen desk and reached for the box of Kleenex next to the phone books. Then I called Ken. He would be picking up Harry after work for dinner and homework at his house. I wanted him to know what was going on. He cried out when I told him about the pencils. I assured him the perpetrators would be dealt with.

The next morning was Ken's Friday to take Harry to school. We had an evenly set morning drop-off schedule and alternated Fridays unless Ken was out of town on business. I only went to the agency Tuesdays through Thursdays, so I occupied my morning with some consulting work for a freelance client I'd taken on. But the hours dragged. It was difficult to keep myself from worrying about the day Harry was having at school. I didn't know if the boys' parents had been called or if Jason and friends were being called into the principal's office that morning. I wanted to trust Dr. Stewart was handling everything in a way that kept Harry out of harm's way. But I still had an underlying fear he might be shoved or kicked in retribution for my call.

After a late lunch I took a drive to the hair salon and spa where Nora worked, one of the younger friends I'd made in the last year. I asked her to distract me with a makeup lesson. I did really need one, and she'd offered more than once. I was still applying what little I did in 1982, when my brother's girlfriend gave me some tips before my wedding. When it was time to pick up Harry, I parked in the drycleaner's lot across the street and walked around to the side door I knew Harry would exit looking for my car.

"So how was your day?" I asked, as we walked side-by-side back to the front of the school.

"Fine," he said in an upbeat tone.

"And how were those boys today?"

"They weren't there. They got suspended."

I was stunned. Why didn't I know that? Dr. Stewart must have called all the parents right after talking to me. I guessed he was too busy dealing some swift Atwater justice. Suspensions! I felt a lilt in my step. This had turned out better than I'd even imagined.

"High five, buddy!" I said, holding up my hand.

Harry slapped my palm as we both grinned accomplishment. We stopped at the curb on traffic-heavy Capitol Drive and waited for a signal from the crossing guard.

"If it weren't for her," Harry said, "you'd have to be Moses to cross this street."

I laughed out loud. "Good one, Harry," I said, with an ease I hadn't felt for two solid weeks.

A letter arrived from the school on Saturday. It was from Dr. Stewart apologizing for the treatment Harry had endured at Atwater. He also informed me that all four boys had been suspended from school for three days. I re-read the letter and then hugged it to my chest. The school had my kid's back. The system had worked.

Three weeks later, the mailman delivered an envelope addressed to Harry in a child's handwriting. In the upper left corner was a return address label for Jason's father. I couldn't imagine why Jason was writing to Harry. I leaned the envelope up against one of the black candleholders in the middle of the glass table. Harry opened the letter after school, and I watched as his eyes moved across the single sheet of lined theme paper.

"Puh," he said, a puff of air escaping his lips. He flicked the letter onto the table and headed for the kitchen.

"What is it?" I asked.

"You can read it," Harry said without turning around.

I quickly skimmed the page. "It's an apology letter," I called.

"He doesn't mean it," Harry said, returning with a snack.

"But I thought all this was settled weeks ago when he and the other boys were suspended. Why is he writing to you now?"

"Because it happened again a couple of days ago."

I was stunned. "It did?! With all the same kids?"

"No, just Jason," Harry said.

He seemed completely unfazed.

"What happened?" I asked, pulling out a chair at the table. I thought the words might sink in better if I were sitting down.

"I told Ms. Prentis, the teacher who sits with Jason every day. After that, he got suspended again."

"There's a teacher who sits next to Jason in class every day?"

"Yup, every day."

"Huh," I replied.

I wanted to step in and help. But scanning Harry's face, he seemed okay. And I realized he'd already helped himself.

"Well, I'm proud of you, Harry," I said, "for handling this on your own."

"Thanks, Mom," he said, lifting his chin with the air of a confident kid.

I told Barbara what had happened when we met for dinner on Harry's Thursday night with Ken.

"This is why actions by parents and teachers are so important," Barbara said over our Asian chicken salads and glasses of white wine at The Knick restaurant downtown. "Kids watch what we do."

"You mean because I called the principal?"

"Because you took action and then something happened," she said. "So Harry wasn't afraid to then do it on his own."

Not only was I proud of Harry, but I felt like I'd earned another mom badge. Harry had learned to stand up for himself and be heard.

I smiled and clinked my glass on Barb's. "To action," I said.

Harry's idea of athletic apparel

From Blue Wig to Hedwig

I stretched out on the couch, propped up two cow-print pillows behind my head, and instantly lost myself in Alice Hoffman's latest book, *The River King*. I didn't look up from the page until Harry entered the living room.

I felt my brows arch to their highest setting. "Harry!" I laughed.

He was wearing the plain pale pink gathered waist dress he'd found at Goodwill for his lunch-lady Halloween costume. A string of pink plastic beads hung around his neck. His eyes batted at me from behind the red plaid frames I'd bought for Heidi years ago when I thought he'd keep his protective glasses on if she were wearing them, too. I recognized the black and gold deco Monet earrings I'd worn for a work portrait the year he was born.

"What?" he asked, putting his hand to his hip as if nothing about his appearance had changed. Then he flashed a huge grin outlined in thick magenta lipstick. "I'm Linda Schneider."

I stretched a broad smile. The name Linda Schneider was somehow funny. "So you want to record something now?"

"Well, if I'm getting all my hair cut off tomorrow, I have to film Linda Schneider's farewell."

I had no idea what prompted Harry's desire for short hair. His thick shoulder-length head of hair had always seemed such a big part of his identity, a feature he'd been so proud of. But as I'd learned with Harry, it was best to just go with the flow and let him keep expressing himself.

"Okay, Linda," I said, sitting up. "Where do you want to be?"

"In the dining room," he said, voice trailing as he ran to the kitchen for the video camera he'd brought home from Ken's.

He had me stand at one end of the dining room table with my back to the windows. He sat at the head of the table opposite me.

"Tell me when you're ready," he said.

I checked the 8mm videotape. I was surprised to see more than half of the sixty-minute cassette had already been used up. I centered his image on the view screen and pressed the red button.

"Action," I said.

"I have some very bad news," Linda began quietly, her face somber. "Me and Texas Jake will not be on the 'Five O'Clock News at Six' or the 'Seven O'Clock News at Eight' anymore."

I steadied the camera with both hands to silence an uncontrollable shoulder laugh.

"We've been transferred to the London News," Linda said, lowering her head with a loud sigh. "Well, to all of my fans out there . . . to all of those girls I've been a role model for, please!" She threw her right hand into the air. "Still watch me on the news. I'll be there, just on a different channel . . . It's sad for me to leave . . .

Now I believe Texas Jake would like to say something. I'll go get him."

Linda got up from the table and I switched off the camera.

"That was really good, Harry. And I love the 'Five O'Clock News at Six' show."

"I'll be right back," he said, bounding up the stairs.

I shook my head. I was impressed with Harry's impromptu on-air monologue. I remembered him play-acting in the wig department at Boston Store and his grand entrance at the family barbeque. Harry was no longer just a little boy in a dress; he was a funny boy in a dress who had finally worked his act to the screen.

Harry returned to the dining room table news desk a few minutes later wearing a tan Panama hat, black wire-rim sunglasses, and a red zip-up shirt with black stripes down the sleeves. I stared at Harry and lost myself for a minute in his concentrated attention to this new character. Every bit of his demeanor had changed. He was definitely no longer Linda Schneider.

"Mom!"

"Sorry, honey." I took my position with the camera and started rolling.

"Hi, y'all. Texas Jake here," he said with a southern drawl. "As Linda probably told ya, me and her are gettin' transferred. And after I just got me a new pair of sunglasses so I could impress y'all! Well the world's a circle, and we've gotta keep on movin'."

I stuck my tongue between my teeth to keep quiet.

"We're probably going to be replaced by some snooty people who don't know what they're talking about," he continued. "Y'all know what I'm sayin'? That sucks. Well, I guess this is goodbye."

123

Harry nodded and I shut off the camera. It was hard to fathom how easily he'd shifted from Linda to Jake.

"Great job on the accent, Harry. And, to be honest, I'm kind of sorry to see Linda and Jake go, too."

"Don't worry, Mom. I'll have new characters for when my hair is short."

After school the next day Harry and I drove downtown for his appointment with Philip at the small salon Ken went to next to the King & I Thai restaurant. Ken had thought Harry would appreciate Philip's leopard-print leggings, six-inch black lace-up platform boots, thick eyeliner and blond hair down to his butt. He was right, and I thought Philip exemplified for Harry the guy who gets to wear whatever he wants to as an adult. I did wish he swept up hair clippings from his floor between customers, though.

Harry explained that he wanted his hair short on the sides and back, and long enough in the front to spike it up.

"You sure about this, Harry?" I asked, as Philip fastened a black nylon cape around his neck.

"Yup," he replied, smiling at my reflection in the large parallelogram-shaped mirror in front of his chair. "I want something new."

I felt a twinge of sadness as the first large clump of Harry's mane hit the floor. I thought of it as a marker of his individuality. I realized I didn't want him to lose any aspect of his unique personality. But if Harry wanted more of a boy cut, who was I to stop him? It just seemed funny to me that years ago I would have preferred his hair short to fit in more with other boys, but now I found myself already missing Harry's singular look.

When Philip finished and was putting some new gel product in Harry's hair that I'd no doubt have to buy, I noticed Harry had the same look he gets before a tetanus vaccination. It stayed with him all the way to the car. He pulled down the passenger side visor, slid open the lighted mirror and scowled.

"You don't like it?" I asked, already knowing the answer.

"No! Philip did *not* listen to what I wanted," he said, pulling up on hairs in the front.

"You'll be able to get it right when you can gel it yourself," I said, trying to sound reassuring.

Harry took a shower when we got home to wash off any loose itchy hairs. I was opening mail at the glass table in the living room when he came out of the downstairs bathroom wrapped in a towel.

"My hair is not only not spikey, it's fluffy!" He didn't wait for any feeble nice-try-mom replies before marching up to his room.

The next afternoon, I could see that the few short peaks he'd managed to carve for himself in the morning had fallen over onto his forehead like spider legs. He slumped into the front seat.

"Mom, you have to take me to get a buzz cut right away. I got laughed at more today than I ever did for having long hair."

"Okay, honey, but I don't think I can get you in to see Phil—"

"No!" he blurted. "I will *never* go back there. Can't you just take me someplace I don't need an appointment? What about Supercuts?"

"I don't know, Harry. Isn't Supercuts just for stylists in training? Maybe if I call Suzanne she can squeeze you—"

"Puh-leeze, Mom, I'm ready to shave my own head. We're making movies this weekend and it can't be with this hair."

Harry's eyes blinked with the urgency of hair despair, a condition I understood from my awkward days of sleeping on brush rollers in junior high.

"Okay," I said. "Supercuts here we come."

Two days later, with his hair sufficiently buzzed off, Harry was home plotting new movie scenes with friends Ian and Max while I ran a few Saturday afternoon errands. While at the end of a long checkout line in Kohl's Food Store, I pulled my cell phone from my purse and dialed home to check on the boys. After four rings, my call went to voice mail. Why didn't Harry pick up? I redialed and hoped it wouldn't be an EMT, policeman, or fire marshal that answered.

"Hello?"

I wondered why Max was on the phone and why "hello" was a question.

"Max, hi, it's Julie. Can I please talk to Harry?"

I heard muffled voices and laughter in the background.

"Can you call back later?" Max asked. "He can't come to the phone right now."

"No, I cannot call back," I said, forgetting I was in the grocery store. The female shopper in front of me, with a child munching Cheerios from a sandwich bag, raised a reprimanding eyebrow. I lowered my voice. "I want to talk to him now, please."

Max covered the phone for a few seconds and then replied, "He's in hair and makeup."

As funny as that sounded coming from a ten-year-old, it was not the answer I wanted to hear. I couldn't believe Harry wasn't coming to the phone. I imagined lipstick and eye shadow smudges on my yellow towels. "He's in hair and makeup?"

"Yeah."

"Listen, Max, is everything okay there?"

"Uh-huh."

"All right. Tell Harry I'll be home soon." I closed my flip phone and decided I wouldn't stop at Goldi's boutique across the street.

Lugging a two-and-a-half gallon plastic jug of Arrowhead Mountain Spring Water in one gloved hand, with several uncooperative bags of dry cleaning sliding on my parka sleeve, I turned my key and pushed open the front door. I heard the boys in the dining room as I slipped off my black Uggs in the tiny vestibule. The interior leaded-glass door cast prism rainbows on the hallway walls as I opened it. Two steps inside, I stopped and stared into the dining room.

Harry and Max sat next to each other, in the same spot Linda Schneider and Texas Jake had said their goodbyes. I gulped when I saw Harry. I wasn't sure if he was supposed to be a boy or a girl. His Army-issue haircut was now the color of a neon lime, accomplished surely with a can of spray dye he had talked me into buying at Bartz's Party Store. In addition to lipstick and eyeliner, he was wearing my retro-styled Harley-Davidson motorcycle jacket. His black boots were crossed on the table, and he was filing his nails with an emery board. Max was dressed in Harry's Nerd Squad t-shirt, and a pair of no-lens glasses with masking tape wrapped around the bridge rested on his nose. Ian held the camera and tape was rolling. I tiptoed past them into the kitchen. I couldn't help but overhear.

"What?!" Harry asked, sounding edgy and tough. "I'm filing my nails. Oh, yeah. I'm supposed to talk."

I heard his feet drop to the floor.

"This show is bogus! I just want to say that right off. We're the new news members, and this geek . . ."

He shoved Max as I walked past for my boots and another trip to the car.

"Hey, Rita!" Sam countered.

He's Rita! Or, she's Rita. I wasn't sure how to refer to Harry in character. Linda was so obviously a girl, but Rita seemed more androgynous. Now that I knew her name, it struck me that Harry had created a very believable butch-girl character. I was in awe of his ability to transform from his ultra-feminine Linda Schneider into someone so markedly different in manner, expression, and tone. It was as if Harry's haircut had given him a new kind of gender freedom that allowed other personalities to emerge.

"You and me, after the show, in the parking lot," Rita barked. "See you then. This show is bogus. I'm getting out of here!" I heard her push away from the table and walk off.

Where had he come up with the word "bogus"? I was so entertained I hated to leave. I zipped my coat as Harry whispered. Then I heard Max say, "And now for some commercials." I headed out the door as the three of them ran upstairs to costumes, hair, and makeup.

A week later, I asked Harry for some birthday gift ideas. The first item on his wish list was "Wigs, Wigs, WIGS!!! (a blue one and other colors)"

"A blue wig?" my brother asked.

"Yep," I told him. "He's making movies these days. And they're pretty good. In addition to writing, directing, and producing, he's also the star."

"Okay," Jack said, reluctantly. "I remember when all he wanted was a blue teddy bear."

"He still has Brambles, Jack. It's his favorite stuffed animal."

For his eleventh birthday my brother sent a bobbed cobalt-blue wig. Harry thought it was one of the best gifts he'd ever gotten. He also received a shoulder-length brassy blond style with bangs from Ken's brother Larry, and Uncle Bobby Baby filled out the spring season collection with a gigantic afro and a crimped Lady Godiva–length wig in ash blond. Harry's costume wardrobe expanded, too, because a Goodwill retail store opened two blocks away from Ken's.

The movie-making continued into sixth grade. Other comical characters Harry paraded in front of the camera included crystal ball fortune-teller Madame Fondue and blond Valley girl Kelly, host of the weekly talk show "Totally Kelly." A live news report that cracked me up described Harry, shrouded in a gray towel and lying on the powder room floor with an empty bottle at his lips, as a nun who had died of alcoholism in Central Park. It struck me that some of the kids' movie scenes were similar to Harry's earlier Barbie doll dramas of broken hearts and untimely deaths. At least the kids were no longer sending Barbie cars careening down our wooden staircase into a deadly whirlpool.

I was impressed by Harry's aptitude for creating and developing so many different characters. While he was still quite the comedian and was comfortable in front of the camera, I couldn't get over how fluidly he moved from one persona to the other. I wondered if his creative range meant he was perhaps a naturally gifted actor. Or maybe these new characters were just the next incarnation of Harry's imaginative play, dolls no longer required.

I was also moved by Harry's passion and dedication to his movie-making, as well as his capacity to work so hard. I wanted to be as excited and focused on my career as he was about his art. But the reality was that the ad agency had changed drastically since the terrorist attacks of September 11. Prospective clients' marketing budgets were frozen and many had a wait-and-see attitude about how the disasters might affect their company's bottom line moving forward. Few marketing directors on my hit list were eager to talk about changing agencies in the wake of such uncertainty. Amid a seemingly endless slowdown, I told the partners I'd be wrapping up my work for them by December. I wasn't sure what I wanted to do next. But I had decided to take a cue from Harry.

Sipping coffee at the kitchen breakfast bar one morning, I read a newspaper story about a local feng shui practitioner. He talked about how the "art of placement" could help individuals gain control over their personal lives and businesses. The words "gain control" set off a spark of enthusiasm that tripped major circuits in my brain. I set down my mug and leaned in closer to the page. According to this expert, feng shui was the ancient Chinese art of using the five elements to "cure" bad energies and activate an environment for harmony and prosperity. The flow of chi was good; clutter was bad. I looked up at my perfectly organized cupboards and countertops. That was it. I could channel my controlling tendencies into a positive place now that I was loosening up on Harry. I could become a clutter expert!

During lunch at my desk, a lengthy internet search located an international feng shui master academy operated by a seventy-eight-year-old Chinese grandmaster in Kuala Lumpur. Classes were offered in cities around the world, with a required final ten-day field study in Malaysia. After talking on the phone with the regional director for North America, headquartered in Miami, I enrolled in Module One. My first three-day class was set for February 2002 in Chicago. To prepare, I bought books on feng shui at the local bookshop and ordered more reading from Amazon.com. I was determined to be a star pupil.

Over the next year and a half, Harry and I both focused on academics. From Day One in my classical feng shui mastery program I learned there was no such thing as a clutter expert; the concept was laughable in Asia. All of the American "pop" feng shui ideas about crystals, mirrors, and Chinese cultural items meant zip in the mathematical formula–based study of authentic feng shui.

Harry had more homework than ever in seventh grade and during the week stayed up studying hours after I went to bed. I woke up thirsty around 1 a.m. one night and squinted when I opened my door to bright lights in the hallway. Harry wasn't in his room. I found him downstairs at the glass table hunched over an art project, an X-Acto knife in his hand. As I got closer, I saw that he was cutting out tiny letters on a stencil.

"Harry, honey, what are you doing up so late?"

"I'm almost done," he said without looking up. "I want to do really well on this piece."

"You know it's okay if you get a B-plus once in a while, right?"

Harry straightened to face me in stunned silence. After the shock of my words wore off, he narrowed his eyes. "No, it's not okay, Mom. I've never gotten a B, and it's not going to happen now."

"Well, I'm just concerned about you. Two of your teachers told me at midyear conferences that sometimes you have trouble staying awake in class."

"I have to get As," he said with determination. "Smart kids don't get picked on, Mom. Nobody ever bothers Matthew Henderson." He turned back to his stencil.

It had never occurred to me that Harry's work ethic was a defensive measure. I hadn't thought about the smart kids not getting picked on. But obviously Harry had witnessed how others respected Matthew, who'd always been at the top of the class. I realized in that moment that Harry was trying to get the same respect. He wasn't about to give up the red and purple hair, spiked leather collar, and Herman Munster boots that were his form of self-expression. He had counterbalanced the way he dressed with being a straight-A student, and I was proud of him for figuring that out.

"All right," I said. "I get it. But please promise me you'll go to bed soon."

"I promise," he said.

I knew there was a chance he'd be up all night, but I wanted to give him his space. As a classical feng shui expert, I knew that energies could be measured. And the five elements of fire, earth, metal, water, and wood related to how environmental energies interacted with an individual's personal energy. Harry was water; I was earth. While I had learned that a little bit of earth could empower water energy, I knew too much earth could destroy it. I needed to stand back from attempts to control Harry's life, especially when it came to knowledge, a strong attribute of water energy.

A few weeks after Harry's thirteenth birthday, he came home from a weekend at Ken's all excited about a new movie he wanted to see.

"It's called *The Rocky Horror Picture Show*, Mom. Can I please go? Please, please, please, please, please?"

To see the transvestite from Transsexual, Transylvania?! Are you kidding me? You're a kid! I'd been to a midnight showing at the Oriental Theatre soon after the movie opened in the mid-seventies. It was campy, outrageous, and fun. People in the audience took props. I'd shaken rice from my hair after the opening wedding scene and laughed when slices of toasted bread flew overhead during the champagne toast. I'd also learned to duck when squirt gun sprinkles accompanied the onscreen rainstorm. I had loved it. I flashed on an image of my crush Tim Curry dressed in a sparkly black lace-up corset, fishnets, and spiked heels doing "The Time Warp" dance.

"Please, Mom, please?" Harry pleaded with his hands held in prayer.

I did a quick inventory of the facts. *Rocky* was a musical, but the content included bisexual lovemaking. It had actually been an educational movie for me back then. There hadn't been any full nudity or explicit sex scenes, but I did vaguely remember Dr. Frank N. Furter hopping from Janet's bed to Brad's and back again to Janet's. But I was out of college then, and Harry had just turned thirteen. He still wore braces.

"What's so special about *Rocky Horror*?" I asked.

"I don't know that much about it," Harry replied. "Katharine said it was about a couple who gets lost, but she couldn't really explain it. I went to the Oriental with her and Dad, and when we came out I saw all these people dressed in crazy costumes waiting in line to see it. And I want to go so bad! Please, please, please can I?"

My gut instinct was to say no. The movie was rated R. It started at midnight and didn't get out until after 2 a.m. Even though his dad lived four blocks from the theater I didn't want him walking home alone so late. But the exhilaration that swept Harry's face describing the people in costume had softened me from giving him a hard "no." I didn't think he really cared about the movie. It was the wildly costumed fringe characters he wanted to experience.

"I'll have to think about it, Harry. I'm not saying no, but I need some time to mull it over."

I wrestled with the decision for weeks, much to Harry's cliff-hanging anticipation. In the end, still against my better judgment, I decided I was not beyond bribery in extreme cases.

"Harry, your dad thinks it's okay for you to see *Rocky Horror*."

"Yes!" Harry shouted with a leap.

"Wait, I'm not finished. I will agree under one condition."

His eyebrows wrinkled.

"You can go to *Rocky* if you promise never to get any piercings or any tattoos."

I could see from Harry's face that he hadn't considered either idea, but I was set on banking for the future.

"I mean it, Harry, *never*. Not now, not in high school, not in college. Promise me."

"Okay, Mom, I promise." Then his whole face smiled and he gave me a hug to match. "Thank you so much!"

Still apprehensive, I pulled my car up on Farewell Avenue across the street from the Oriental Theatre at 11:45 p.m. What was I doing dropping Harry off this late by himself? I eyed the older teenagers and twenty-somethings in line under the lit marquee that read "Rocky Horror Tonight!" They all looked so old compared to Harry, who looked like a kid. I spotted a woman with a gold glitter jacket and top hat, another in a strapless red satin dress with a huge tattoo on her back, and a young man wearing a long turquoise cape. I stayed where I was until Harry entered the theater, just in case he got turned away for a ticket. Then I reluctantly pulled away from the curb and turned the corner, headed for home.

While waiting at the traffic light on North Avenue, I wondered if Harry had found the friends from high school he said would give him a ride to Ken's or if he was sitting by himself. I cringed imagining flasks of alcohol being shared among a rowdy crowd, couples making out and some college kid next to Harry passing him a joint. When the light changed to green, instead of going straight I turned left, back in the direction of the theater. I wanted to know what was going on in there.

I felt lucky to find a parking place in the small public lot behind Von Trier's Pub on the corner across from the Oriental. I locked the car, shoved my hands in my jacket pockets, and walked briskly across the street to the theater box office. I opened the heavy ornate door to the main theater and was surprised the house lights were still on. I put my head down and quickly ducked into a seat at the end of a back row, hopeful Harry hadn't seen me sneak in. There was a lineup of people in *Rocky Horror* character costumes standing in front of the screen on the theater stage. It appeared to be some sort of contest. The crowd was well behaved and I didn't smell any weed. I stayed only fifteen minutes into the movie and left as quietly as I had entered, fears of exposure to debauchery subdued.

I couldn't fall asleep that night. I was sure Harry was fine inside the theater, but I felt my heart accelerate at the thought of him getting home safely after two in the morning. I waited until nine o'clock to call Ken's. Katharine answered and confirmed that Harry was sound asleep in his bed. I hung up the phone and exhaled an audible sigh with relief. Harry was growing up and there was nothing I could do about that.

By the end of eighth grade Harry had a regular posse who accompanied him to the Oriental on *Rocky Horror* nights. He now dressed in elaborate costumes and encouraged his friends to do the same. Because Ken lived so close to the theater, they got ready at his house. And after only one pre-*Rocky* episode left my upstairs sink filled with open pots of iridescent eye shadows and the bathroom rug covered with enough glitter to look like Aladdin's magic carpet, I had insisted they get dressed at Ken's.

That summer, the items Harry bought shopping at Goodwill, Closet Classics, and the vintage shops on Brady Street expanded to include costume-worthy garments and whatever inexpensive high heels he could find in his size. I was amazed by his taste and style, as well as his resourcefulness in putting outfits together. I thought about asking him to be my personal shopper.

Harry burst through the back door one August afternoon flushed from the heat and wearing a super-sized grin. "Look what I found!" he said, reaching into a white plastic bag.

I shut off the kitchen tap and set down a colander of fresh-rinsed blueberries. When I turned around I was surprised to see him holding up a small cream-colored women's cardigan. It didn't look like something Harry would wear, but I held back from commenting. Harry's fashion sense was still a notch up from my own.

"That looks tiny, honey."

"I know, Mom. It's supposed to. I'm going to be Janet at the next *Rocky Horror Picture Show*. I'm going to enter my first costume contest this time."

"You are?" I asked, my heart fluttering a little.

"Yeah, the next show has a beach theme." Then his eyes widened like a kid who'd just been given his own pony. "Wait till you see the really cute floral-print bikini I found at Yellow Jacket!"

Oh my God. You're going to be wearing a bikini?

"Let's see it," I said, infusing a dash of upbeat inflection in my voice to counter the scary visual in my head of Harry wearing a bikini to the Oriental. This wasn't just the dress-up box anymore, or creating costumed characters for his funny home movies, this was my son making a costumed stage debut in the outside world. He would be up there in front of a packed theater of strangers.

Then I realized Harry was going to be competing, and I wouldn't be there to see him. I thought about asking him if I could go, but the last thing he needed was to know his mother was in the audience.

"Oh, I didn't buy the bikini today. It's at Dad's."

I hid my disappointment with a default smile. "That's okay. What does it look like?"

"Well, there's a bullet-shaped bra top with little cones," he said, standing back to pose and gesticulate the rundown. "The bottoms are high-waisted with a metal zipper in the back. It's definitely vintage 1960s, maybe early 1970s. Oh, and I found the perfect white floppy hat."

Harry described his costume with so much pride that I didn't even care he had just referred to clothes from my high school years as vintage. He'd found exactly the items he wanted to make Susan Sarandon's Janet character his own. I was proud of him for pulling it all together, even if he hadn't needed me to take him shopping.

Harry cinched first place for his Janet portrayal and won two tickets to see the Skylight Music Theatre's local production of *Hedwig and the Angry Inch*. "Huh," I'd thought. Harry's education about transsexuals was about to be furthered by another rock musical. Ken and I had seen John Cameron Mitchell's movie version of his off-Broadway show when it was first released in 2001, but never the play. I was eager to know what Harry would make of a story about a so-called botched sex-change operation.

"So, what did you think?" I asked him after he'd seen the show with a girlfriend from school.

"It changed my life," he said.

I was taken aback by his answer. Harry's clothes, hair, makeup, and attitude had all changed already in real life. I tried to imagine what it was about the play that had moved him so deeply. Was it the character of Hedwig who so defiantly didn't care what anyone else thought? I wanted to know more.

"Really, how so?" I asked.

"Well, first, the music was so good."

I remembered the "Origin of Love" about the world being filled with sets of children of three sexes before the gods broke them apart. It was a sad and beautiful song about how love in the world was meant to be. My eyes had watered when that song played in the movie and I'd thought of Harry. "What else?" I wanted to know.

"Oh, the hair and makeup. And Hedwig was a rock star!"

Harry didn't say anything about the sex change or why Hedwig attempted it. Still, I couldn't help but think he'd identified with a character so liberated and immensely free to be her authentic self. Then it dawned on me that both Hedwig and Frank N. Furter were male performers who had openly celebrated their female identities. They had connected Harry to the world in ways I never could, and he was embracing that world. I liked the image of Harry with his arms wrapped around the globe. I felt like I learned from him all the time about confidence and self-esteem. He was so different from the awkward, insecure kid I had been the summer before high school.

That night, as I put on mascara in front of the bathroom mirror, I imagined Harry doing the same thing over at Ken's. And I realized that if I hadn't let him go to *Rocky Horror* in the first place he might not be feeling the joy he did right now. I felt one corner of my mouth turn up; I had done something good for Harry. A year and a half earlier I'd made a decision that most parents probably wouldn't have made, one that was now helping my self-esteem soar a little bit, too. I winked at my reflection, proud that I'd come so far.

Christmas at Harry's dad's house

Ken Hanson

Harry Decides

I can walk in heels better than any of my girlfriends," Harry said, crumbling saltines into his matzo ball soup at Benji's Deli.

We'd been talking about his upcoming trip to New York with his dad. Harry planned to take his *Rocky Horror* Dr. Frank N. Furter costume, which included a pair of black patent leather platform heels.

I knew Harry was probably right about his proficiency in heels. I couldn't recall any of the girls at his eighth grade graduation wearing even low pumps. Then I flashed on images of Harry as a toddler playing with the heels stacked in boxes on my closet floor.

"Well, you've been wearing them since you were three," I said, with a hint of pride.

Harry smiled.

Our waitress returned with a plate of Super Hoppel Poppel for Harry and a half sandwich of corned beef and chopped liver for me. I reached for the yellow squirt bottle of mustard, while Harry mixed up the scrambled eggs, fried salami, and veggie concoction in front of him.

"Mom, I think I'm bisexual."

What? Really? Bisexual?

The word ricocheted inside my head. I didn't know how to respond. Did this mean Harry was really gay, but just didn't know it yet? It was 2004, years before the spectrum of gender identity was acknowledged as a real thing and before bisexuality was taken seriously. I didn't know anyone who was bisexual. And I'd always heard that bisexual was just a stage someone went through before figuring out they were really gay. I certainly didn't want to put any of that on Harry. But if he was just noodling his way to gay, I didn't know how long it would take before he knew. Then my mind jumped to him dating now that he was in high school. I gulped back a fear of him being rejected.

"Okay," I said, pressing the top piece of bread back onto my sandwich. "Tell me what makes you think that."

"Well, I'm attracted to both girls and boys."

"Do you think you're attracted to each in the same way?"

He thought for a moment. "Well, I think I'm probably more attracted to girls intellectually."

Harry did have more girlfriends than boyfriends. Even in kindergarten he was usually the only boy invited to girls' birthday parties. I'd watched him thrive in those close friendships. He trusted and loved his girlfriends and by first grade had crushes on redheads. I remembered that in sixth grade the shy blond Kayla had received extra attention. At the end of that school year, he'd come home from a walk with her carrying two small, entwined teddy bears, one red; the other one white. When I asked him if he liked Kayla as a "girlfriend" girlfriend, he shrugged and told me they'd kissed on the beach. I took that as a yes. But by the start of seventh grade they were just friends. A week ago he'd gone to the Sadie Hawkins freshman dance with Simone, the super-smart and waifish girl who'd played Patty opposite his Eugene in the eighth grade production of *Grease*. I was sure they had crushes on each other. But I didn't know about any special guy in his life.

I hadn't discussed Harry's sexual orientation with him before. He knew I had friends who were "boyfriend and boyfriend." In preschool he'd told me that his classmate Jacob had two moms, so he knew what the possibilities were for couples. At eleven, he'd asked me how lesbians had sex if there was no penis. After explaining that women had fingers and tongues, I'd told him he could probably figure out how gay man had sex, too. But I wondered what prompted Harry to consider himself bisexual. Then I flashed to the Dr. Frank N. Furter character. The scientist-doctor had created his ideal muscleman hunk Rocky, but still later that night seduced virgins Janet and Brad. And Eddie's sequin-clad groupie Columbia had been plenty touchy-feely with the ruby-lipped maid Magenta during one of the musical numbers. I knew Harry had to discover his sexuality on his own, but now that he was still thinking about it, I thought maybe I could help him close the gap on knowing.

"Is there one sex that arouses you more?" I asked.

As soon as my words filled the space between us I wished I could have sucked them back into my mouth. *Jesus H. Christ, Julie!* Harry had just shared highly personal information with me. I hated myself for responding like a nosy neighbor. I was his mother for God's sake! Did I really think I was going to help him figure out his sexual orientation right then and there over Hoppel Poppel?

Harry blushed the same scarlet as our translucent water glasses. "I don't think that's any of your business."

"You're right. It is none of my business. I'm sorry, honey."

I felt ashamed for prying and thanked my lucky stars Harry had stopped me. I remembered Harriet Lerner's term "gender flexible" from *The Mother Dance*, which had been a great placeholder for me when he was in middle school. And if sexual orientation was flexible too, so what? It was Harry's to explore for himself. I inhaled and reminded myself that all I needed to focus on was his happiness and security.

"Listen, Harry, whomever you end up with will be lucky to have you as a partner."

A broad smile stretched across his face. "Thanks, Mom."

I looked with approval at the handsome, teenaged face of the kid I loved more than anything. Then I remembered the world beyond Benji's back booth, to the reality of promiscuity, STDs, and HIV. All of a sudden I was back in L.A. at my friend Harry's last party, where he died to escape the brutality of AIDS. There was no fucking way in hell I was going to let that happen to my son. I was going to make damn sure that he outlived me. I didn't want to scare Harry, but I needed him to be smart and aware.

"And, Harry," I said, "you have to use condoms. For everything."

"I know."

"I mean it, Harry, for *everything.*"

"Mom, I know! Don't worry."

He had no idea how useless "Don't worry" was following a discussion of condoms. I didn't think Harry was sexually active. He was, after all, only fourteen, and I thought he'd tell me if he were serious about someone. But I didn't want to be naïve. A friend in Cincinnati had told me two years earlier there'd been a scandal at a local junior high when it was discovered some of the girls were giving boys blowjobs. I'd been shocked speechless when I learned the girls thought it was no big deal, because blowjobs weren't "going all the way." I didn't think anything like that was going on among Harry's crowd of overachievers. Still, I didn't want him having sex too young. And I got sad thinking about the day his heart would be broken for the first time.

I was distracted from thinking about Harry's sexuality by some new turns of events. George Bush winning a second term was just half of it. I left for Miami the Friday after the election knowing I'd be missing all of the weekend-only performances of *Little Shop of Horrors*. My private Xuan Kong feng shui course had been scheduled in July. I'd been asked to join the consultation company's executive team, and I had to be there. I wanted to be there. Luckily, I did get to see my nonspeaking Bum Number One at the dress rehearsal Thursday night, but it wasn't the same as opening night. I vowed never to be away for another one of Harry's shows. The day after I returned from my week away Harry told me he'd attended an AFS study-abroad presentation at the high school. He wanted to spend his sophomore year in Europe.

"I thought the AFS program was for juniors," I said.

"Usually it is, but I want to go next year," he replied in earnest. "You only have to be fifteen. I have it all figured out."

Harry's face was set with determination, but I was wary. The program was set up for sixteen-year-olds, and he was only fourteen. He'd be fifteen soon, but that seemed too young to be moving to another country for school.

"Okay, explain it to me."

"Well, if I go as a junior, I'll miss taking AP classes that year. And in—"

"What are AP classes?" I asked.

"Advanced Placement. And in AFS you don't get grades, you only get credits. I plan to get straight As in high school, Mom, and I want to take as many AP classes as I can, especially art."

I knew Harry had wanted to excel in class and get good grades to fend off bullying in middle school, but this was taking his studies to another level. He had figured out his entire four-year curriculum. I wished I could have been that driven as a high-school freshman. All I'd cared about at his age was keeping my hair straight, getting a separate phone line for my room, and passing my temporary driver's license test. In my next life I wanted to come back as Harry.

"What country do you want to go to? And which semester?"

"Oh, I want to go for the whole year. It will look better on my college applications," he said. "I wanted to go to the Netherlands, but you have to be seventeen for that program. So my next choice is Spain, because I already speak Spanish. It's a very popular AFS country, so I have to do early application and get it in by the end of January."

"But that's only two months away, Harry."

"I know. I can do it."

One night during Christmas vacation, I passed the entryway stairs as Harry came down from working on his AFS application online. He flashed a Cheshire-cat grin in my direction. I was sure he'd beat his own deadline.

"Did you finish?" I asked.

"Almost," he replied and then, still grinning, paused at the bottom of the stairs. "Mom, I'm gay."

I smiled as my emotions rocketed to happy, and tingles tickled my scalp. I felt the urge to applaud. Harry knew! I'd been nervous so often when Harry was younger that he might be gay. I'd thought his being gay would only make his adult life miserable. I'd projected all of the worst possible outcomes, like hatred and slurs from bigots and discrimination on the job. And now, ten years later, I was relieved to just finally have the answer. My kid was gay! I felt pride and excitement for him. Harry knew who he was. He'd shared it with me as happy news. And best of all, I knew he felt good about himself.

"Oh, okay, honey. That's great!" I returned to the glass table where floor plans for the acupuncture clinic I was working on were spread out. I sat down, but couldn't concentrate on energy maps. I was focused on whether or not there was a certain someone in Harry's life.

Harry rounded the corner from the kitchen with a tall yellow Tupperware glass of orange juice.

"So, Harry," I called. "Have you met someone?"

"Yes," he beamed. "His name is Brett."

Oh, my God! Harry had a boyfriend. I wanted to know everything. "Do I know him?" I asked. "Does he go to Shorewood?"

"I met him online."

I felt the blood drain from my face. I imagined a sweaty middle-aged pedophile sitting in front of his computer in boxer shorts posing as a teenager in online chat rooms hoping to lure some unsuspecting kid into meeting him at the mall.

"Oh," I said, trying to keep my tone setting on innocently interested. "How old is he, honey?"

"He's a year older than me. He lives in San Francisco."

Whew! No meetings at the mall anytime soon. "Well, I hope you're careful in those chat rooms, Harry. Some people aren't who they say they are."

Harry laughed. "I know that, Mom. I'm not a little kid. We met on LiveJournal. It's cool."

When second semester started, Harry still stayed up until all hours doing his homework in front of the computer on the third floor. He didn't talk much about Brett, but I knew Harry kept an AOL Instant Messenger window open on his screen to chat with friends while working. I was sure he had a separate window open for private conversations with Brett. Harry and his friends all seemed to talk only online. So when I heard him on the phone behind closed doors after midnight, I knew he was probably speaking with Brett in San Francisco, where the time was two hours behind.

Soon after his fifteenth birthday in March 2005, Harry heard from AFS that he would indeed be studying in Spain that fall. He flushed with excitement at the news, but some thoughts about Spain made me cringe. I knew Picasso's home of flamenco, bullfighting, and tapas would be beautiful, but it was the Spanish Inquisition and Franco's forty-year dictatorship that had me wondering how Harry would be accepted there. I hadn't talked to him about how cruel the world could be, how the kids who were bullies in fifth grade could grow up to be teenage bullies anywhere in the world. I couldn't bring myself to tell Harry some people would hate him for being gay, and not just in Spain.

When I asked him about the country's policies towards homosexuality, he told me that same-sex marriage was legal there. "Really?" I'd asked. It was hard for me to believe that was true. I felt my scrunched shoulders lower a notch, but knew AFS often sent kids into smaller towns. I equated low population with conservative views.

I didn't get much of a chance to dwell on fears of whether or not Harry would be accepted for who he was in Spain, because I was soon distracted by his request to visit Brett in June. Conveniently the Shorewood High School Choir had booked a performance in San Francisco a few days after the school year ended. Harry wanted to visit Brett before returning home. According to Harry, his dad was fine with him spending a couple of extra days at Brett's. Harry knew Ken was his more lenient parent, so I wasn't surprised he'd asked his dad first. I'd been the one who'd fretted since Day One about Harry wearing his glasses, wanting to be Wendy, and dressing in skirts outside the house. Ken had, after all, given his approval before I did for Harry to see the midnight showing of *Rocky Horror* in seventh grade. But this was sleeping over at his boyfriend's house, halfway across the country; the same boyfriend who had just sent him a handmade silver ring.

"What are you so worried about?" Ken asked, when I called to chastise him for being so permissive.

Apparently kids in the suburb of Menomonee Falls hadn't taken advantage of "my parents aren't home" the way my friends and I had in high school. I figured kids were even "faster" these days.

"I just don't want him having sex yet. He's only fifteen, for God's sake."

"Oh, Julie, you don't know that's what's going to happen."

Yeah, right.

"But if you think they're going to be left unsupervised the whole time," Ken continued, "give Brett's mom a call and talk to her."

Harry rolled his eyes when I told him why I wanted Brett's home number. But Brett's mom Christine didn't make me feel at all like I was being paranoid to ask about her schedule. Her voice put me at ease immediately. She was a single mom, too, and I imagined us being friends if we lived in the same city. We emailed a couple of times after that. I sent her details about picking up Harry at the airport before the rest of the choir boarded a plane back home. And I explained I'd given the choir director Mr. Heath a letter saying Harry had my permission to be picked up by his "Aunt Christine," as the school could only release a student to a family member. She was going to have to show her ID. And even though I couldn't bring myself to ask where Harry would be sleeping, I still worried about her son getting too intimate with mine.

I wanted to remind him again to be vigilant and smart about entering into his first serious relationship. Harry had learned about safe sex in Atwater's fifth-grade sex education class, but that was four years ago. I wasn't sure how well he'd been paying attention to the consequences of STDs and AIDS. I didn't know if he really understood how serious that was. Harry was an intelligent kid, but I still felt like I had to keep him on his guard about unprotected sex. He hadn't seen friends die firsthand. After all, he was still just a kid. Before dropping Harry off at school for the bus to the airport, I thought for a second about telling him to sleep with all his clothes on. But I didn't. I wanted to have confidence that Harry would stay smart and make good decisions. I knew some of the stores where Harry shopped kept fishbowls filled with condoms near the cash register. I could only hope he'd grab a handful of freebies before this trip.

Harry ended up staying with his boyfriend for two nights. And because it was over Father's Day weekend, Ken made plans to fly out to San Francisco. He picked up Harry from Brett's, and the two of them spent a few father-son days together hanging out in the city. Harry came home with the same expression as the smiley-face symbol.

"I'm so glad you had such a great time with Brett," I said. "What did you guys do?"

"We hung out at his house mostly," Harry replied. "They have a pool."

"You didn't go anywhere?"

"We went to the mall, did a little shopping. Brett took me out to a really fancy dinner, and we went to a bistro that was cute but not as fancy. His mom made us breakfast in the morning."

Oh, jeez. Don't go there, Julie.

"And how did things go when Brett's mom picked you up?" I asked, switching gears on my anxiety.

"Oh, yeah, that. Well, Mr. Heath knew she wasn't my aunt."

"What?" I couldn't believe it. Brett's mom had been so on board. I felt my eyelids blink in rapid succession as I imagined the *Shorewood Herald*'s headline, "Mom Lies about Family in Letter to H.S. Administrator."

"It's because Brett was waiting at the airport when we all got there, and he gave me a big ol' kiss on the mouth. It wasn't very cousinly."

"Great, Harry," I said. "I can't wait until I have to sort that out with the school."

I hoped the Aunt Christine letter situation would just blow over, but soon I received a terse email from the choir director informing me he could have lost his job by releasing Harry to someone who wasn't a family member. He advised me that in the future, only a parent would be able to pick up a student from a field trip in another city. I still thought a parent's permission should suffice.

By the beginning of August, Harry told me he and Brett were feeling the strain of the miles. They were still close, but had agreed to see other people. I told him long-distance relationships sucked and were hard even for people my age. Soon after, he started going out with another older boy named Jonathan, who'd been accepted by early decision to Brown University. I remembered Jonathan from Harry's family orientation assembly at the high school. He'd been a junior, and was one of the student council members onstage in the auditorium talking about the school's gay-straight alliance,

SHARE. Harry and I had joked about the name, because it was a homophone with Cher, whom Harry adored.

I had liked what Jonathan contributed to the panel on stage that night, but now I resented him. Why would he start a relationship with my kid just weeks before leaving for college? I was convinced that another long-distance romance so soon after Brett was going to break my son's heart. I consoled myself thinking at least Harry was going out with a guy who was as smart and good-looking as he was. And Jonathan was Jewish. I thought it funny that I'd never cared about dating Jewish guys, but now I liked the idea that Harry was.

I wanted to stay close to Harry and be involved in his life, but I knew I needed to step back in the love department. I had to get used to the idea that Harry was becoming an adult. I was sure he longed for the same freedoms I'd been so desperate for in high school, even as a sophomore. I wanted everything to work out for Harry and his summer love, even if they would each be traveling to new schools, friends, and experiences. I knew I had to trust Harry and his choices. I needed to be a mom who could let go.

A style all his own

The Pain in Spain

Harry's cell phone number appeared on my caller ID. He'd only been gone a day, but the sound of his voice had the same effect on me as a tranquility tank. I knew these calls would be rare in the months ahead.

"Everything is going great, Mom! I met a ton of friends who are all going different places."

"I'm so glad, honey. That's really wonderful. Do you have a family yet?"

We'd received word two weeks before Harry left for Spain that he'd be living with a family near Barcelona. Then only days before his pit stop in D.C. for a national student orientation, AFS sent an alert that the family had backed out of hosting a student. The email apologized for the last-minute change and assured us they were working nonstop to find another host. I'd been dumbstruck. I was supposed to send my fifteen-year-old kid to Spain without knowing where he'd be living?

When I called my AFS liaison, who I was sure was a college intern, she'd told me this wasn't unusual. Nailing down host families sometimes went down to the wire, and other kids headed for Spain were in the same situation as Harry. I didn't know why she'd thought knowing other kids were in Harry's homeless boat would make me feel better. I'd hung up the phone believing that AFS Spain was an organization of incompetent imbeciles.

"Oh, yeah, that's why I called," Harry said. "I'm going to stay in a suburb of Madrid with a lady named Valerie and her son Alvaro who's eighteen."

God bless the Niña, the Pinta, and Santa María! Harry had a family.

"But they're only a 'welcome' family," he continued, "which means I can only stay with them for two weeks while they find me a permanent family."

Dammit, what?! "Welcome family" sounded like emergency family to me. And Harry was supposed to start school soon. So now he was going to have to switch families and change schools, too? I was pissed. At least I could erase the mental images of Harry sleeping under a blanket on the couch at the AFS headquarters in Madrid.

"Well, it's progress, Harry," I said, feigning calm. "Be sure to email me her phone number and your address when you get there, okay?"

"I will. And can you please send my parka, my yearbook, and some microwave mac and cheese?"

My next contact about Spain arrived via email from a yahoo.es account. It was Harry's Spanish mom, Valerie. I clicked on it and was surprised to see a full-page letter. I pushed aside my desktop keyboard and quickly scanned the tiny type.

"AFS has me on their list in case they need temporary shelter for students . . . I have been in touch with them throughout these two weeks to know what was happening with Harry's future host family . . . There are three more students apart from Harry who don't have a host family . . . I was supposed to hear by today of two possibilities for him . . . the manager is on her way to a general meeting in north Spain . . . hadn't left any message for me . . . I am going to write a very critical report to the national AFS office . . ."

I felt little flashing lights flip on in my head. Harry was being left hanging by AFS and now his mom in Spain was worried about him being in a temporary placement, too. She wasn't the only one who'd be writing to AFS. I read on.

" . . . awkward situation . . . his real integration into Spanish life is being unnecessarily delayed . . . although he is a very mature person, he is nonetheless only 15 . . ."

I wanted to hug her. She was looking out for Harry and was prepared to defend him to the top of the study program's messed-up hierarchy. She knew the person in charge of all the volunteers, who had confirmed that night that AFS Spain was overwhelmed by work and relied on volunteer young people who don't fully assume their so-called job. So they relied on former AFSers like her to help to sort out the situation. I read on.

" . . . there is no definitive family yet, although they are interviewing a few."

She asked me to put pressure on my local AFS contact. She gave me the number of AFS Madrid and also her home telephone.

Tapping all of my fingers on the arms of my chair, I debated whom to call first. It was just before noon my time, so I called Harry's mom in Spain. She spoke fluent English with a French accent. Her voice was warm, kind, and admittedly frustrated. She said no one at AFS was being helpful. I empathized with her and thanked her repeatedly for taking Harry in and remaining so patient. In the end, she agreed to let Harry stay longer than she'd originally offered.

After we hung up, I stretched my arms over my head, clasped my hands to crack my fingers and let my head hang back. I felt the tension in my spine loosen. I sat up, dialed AFS National and left a message for my contact Courtney, who was on the phone with another parent. I imagined phones ringing like the switchboard at a 911 dispatcher, all calls from moms whose kids were in Spain. Next I searched online for international gift delivery companies and arranged for Valerie to receive a goody basket the size of Texas.

She sent another email five days later. Harry was enrolled in school and, according to her, enjoying it. She explained that regardless of where his eventual host family lived, it was easier to transfer schools than to register late. Then I learned that the three families they had lined up had all fallen through. She hadn't told Harry that yet. My spirit and shoulders slumped thinking of Harry expecting to hear any moment about which of those families would take him. I leaned closer to the screen for her last lines:

"They have told me that there is now a family in Seville. You see, Spain is not an easy country to find host families. I am afraid their only mistake is to accept too many students. But I am sure there will be a solution soon. Anyway, maybe by Tuesday, AFS Milwaukee should check again. . . . Don't worry! Your son is in good hands. Valerie"

I drummed my fingers on my collarbone. I was relieved to know she was still looking out for Harry, but I was now livid that my first suspicions of AFS Spain as a dis-organization were being confirmed. She and I were both on the phone with AFS multiple times over the next few days only to be assured by so-called administrators on two continents that they would soon have a family for Harry. I moved into corporate powerhouse mode, taking on the persona of Joan Collins as Alexis Carrington Colby Dexter Colby from the '80s TV show *Dynasty*, and listed all of the facts that proved their bungling of Harry's placement. I demanded that a host family for Harry be found immediately. But then I felt silly. I knew I was powerless to actually make anything happen. So I fantasized setting up camp in the lobby of AFS Madrid with a tent and sleeping bags for Harry and me until a family was secured. But I knew that was ridiculous; Harry would kill me. Plus, I had scheduled a Colorado mountain biking trip and some work with a feng shui colleague there for a couple of businesses in Breckenridge.

Valerie's final email arrived while I was still out west. It had been a month since she first welcomed Harry into her home. I calculated the time difference to just before midnight her time. Her message was brief.

"I wanted to write to let you know that this morning I called AFS Madrid and found out that they still haven't found a family for Harry. I have waited, but now I have a friend coming from Paris to visit. So I will drive Harry tomorrow afternoon to AFS office in Madrid and they will have to take care of him. I have discussed the situation with Harry and he understands. I do feel sorry for him . . ."

I closed my eyes and dropped my face into my hands. What the hell was going on in Spain? I learned from Harry that it was indeed actual hell that was going on in Spain. He sounded defeated when he called from the AFS office to say he'd be spending the next week in downtown Madrid, at the apartment of an AFS volunteer's friend.

"And it's weird, Mom," he said in a hushed voice. "There's a look-book in the lobby here with photos of all the kids who need families, and my picture's not in it."

My eyebrows wrinkled. That did seem odd. But if staff members were all on the phone for hours as Harry had described, calling everyone they knew to find host families, maybe they didn't keep up with lobby materials.

"Maybe those are just old photos, Harry."

"No, they're not," said Harry, incredulous. "There's another boy I know who needs a family, and his picture is in here."

What the fuck?! They didn't have a family for Harry, they're calling around desperately, and yet they don't include his photo in the lobby book? I knew it might be difficult finding a family for Harry; he was a vegetarian and allergic to cats, dogs, and cigarette smoke. But all of that was made clear on his application. I started to grind my teeth. Were they treating my creative and colorful son differently because they thought he was gay?

"Listen, just tell them to do it," I instructed, being careful not to misdirect my anger at AFS onto my stranded child. "There's no excuse for your photo not to be in that book. Clearly they don't know what they're doing."

Subsequent reports from Harry came via email. He was sleeping on the couch in this second "welcome" family's one-bedroom apartment. The young couple's only bathroom was attached to their bedroom, and they slept until 3 p.m. They didn't give Harry a key so he couldn't leave before they awoke, which on several occasions forced him to pee in the sink. The week after that, despite his noted allergies to smoke, he was placed with Family Number Three, where the dad was a heavy cigar smoker. According to Harry, he only removed the smelly chewed-up stubs from his mouth to eat or hack up sizeable chunks of his lungs.

I woke up each morning to thoughts of Harry being handed off like an unwanted orphan. I drank coffee, but had no appetite for anything but my cuticles. I lost weight. My dermatologist diagnosed a pimply rash on the back of my neck as neuro-folliculitis, an inflammation of the hair follicles caused by anxiety. I left his office with the advice to alternate applications of Neosporin and hydrocortisone and not to worry so much.

Harry called me from the AFS office after being freed from the smoke chamber to confer about Family Number Four.

"They found a family for me east of Madrid, with two kids in college," he said in a low monotone.

"Thank God, Harry!" I said, flopping backwards onto my bed. "Finally! I was getting ready to come over there and get you."

"But I'd have to go to a Catholic school run by nuns," he whispered. "The same school their boys went to."

I snapped upright at the waist. "What? Why? AFS guarantees public school!"

"I know," Harry answered. "That's why I need your permission. The town's public school didn't have room for any more kids. The next closest one is an hour and a half away, and they don't want to drive me. It's even longer if I have to take two buses."

I got up and began pacing the wood floor in a U-shape around my bed. This was crazy. Ken considered himself a fallen Catholic, and Harry's only tie to religion was my influence of casual Judaism. I wouldn't send him to any religious school in the United States, so why would I agree to a parochial school in Spain of all places? But Harry needed a family placement in order to be in school. And he needed to be in school for the credits required to graduate from Shorewood. I took a long, deep breath. I decided to leave it up to Harry.

"Tell me how you feel about it."

"Well, I asked if corporal punishment was allowed, and they said no," he replied, "so I guess I'm okay with it."

I chuckled. "Good question, Harry. I wouldn't have thought to ask that. But I guess you never know with Spanish nuns."

"The school is run by Italian nuns, Mom."

What? As if nuns from the Spanish Inquisition weren't enough, now they were Italian? As far as I was concerned, that was only one step away from the pope. I imagined Harry as a young Federico Fellini, surrounded by a swarm of sour-faced nuns in starched white habits and oversized winged headdresses.

"Are you sure about this, Harry?"

"Honestly, Mom, if I don't take this family, Madalena, who runs the office, said she didn't know how long it would take to find another one."

My next phone call from Harry came two weeks after he'd started at the Catholic school, where his new schedule included religion class.

"Mom! They're trying to convert me!" he shouted into the phone, sounding panicked. "I'm not kidding! Sister Clementina handed out these cards of people with yellow circles around their heads. And—"

"You mean the saints?" I remembered Sally Polinski, the pretty blond baton twirler on my block growing up, showing me those cards after her first communion.

"I don't know what they are, Mom, but she gave me one of a guy who was Jewish and then saw Jesus and then went blind and was finally *beheaded!*"

"Well, that's ridiculous," I said. "And so is the fact they're even making you take that religion class in the first place."

"I was hoping it would be a survey class, but no! It's all about Jesus being like the broken pieces of an indestructible vase, or something."

This can't be happening!

I put my hand to my forehead hoping to pull some psychic solution from my brain. With each call from Harry I felt myself edge closer to a state of maternal vengeance. Harry was with his fourth family in two months. And now some medieval anti-Semitic nuns were persecuting him? I seethed hatred for AFS Spain, but I needed to calm myself and be the voice of reason. I brushed the bangs off my forehead and cleared my throat.

"Listen, Harry, talk to your Spanish mom. Ask her to get you out of religion class. You said the family's not at all religious, so she's not going to care. I'm sure she'll do that for you."

"Yeah, okay. I'll ask her."

I hung up the phone and sat immobilized on the chair outside my bedroom. I never got headaches, but now felt a tight pulsing on the left side of my forehead. How much could one kid take? How much more could I take?

A week later, I was leaned up against the kitchen counter sipping coffee and paging through the morning paper when the home phone rang. It was Harry.

"Mom?" he asked, his voice quavering.

I stood at attention and pressed the phone to my ear. "Harry, what is it? Are you okay?"

"Today was the most horrible day of my life," he said softly, his voice still shaky. He sniffled, and I knew he'd been crying.

Every nerve ending in my body flared. I made a fist. Why was Harry crying? Who had hurt my baby? I took a deep breath.

"Oh, no, Harry. What happened? Tell me."

He explained he'd been in science class before lunch when he got called down to the Mother Superior's office. He assumed it was to find out he'd be going to the library during religion class. His mom there had completely understood and talked to the head nun at school about getting him out of it.

"The Mother Superior, who doesn't speak a word of English, started off asking me about my problem with religion class. But then she paused and told me she'd been hearing some things, personal things about me. 'Have you been telling people about yourself?' she asked me. I pretended I didn't know what she was talking about."

He stopped to blow his nose.

"She said, 'I heard that you like boys.' And I said, 'Oh, that. Yeah.' Then she gave me a death stare for about five minutes before speaking again. She wanted to know why I would say something like that. I told her that's the way I am, and that I wasn't embarrassed about it."

"Good for you, Harry," I said. "But I'm surprised you told anyone you were gay, given you're at a Catholic school."

"I *didn't* tell anyone, Mom. I decided before I left that I wasn't going to say anything, but if someone asked me I wasn't going to lie. And the girls figured it out in like five minutes."

"Okay, honey."

I was so proud of him for being true to who he was, but I didn't like where the conversation was headed. My stomach began to feel unsettled. I knew it wasn't the coffee.

"Then the Mother Superior said, 'Society is very cruel, Harry. Do you know that?' And I told her that all the kids had been really nice to me. But she wasn't talking about the other kids; she was talking about their parents. She said there were parents of kids at the school who didn't want their child in class with a homosexual."

"Oh my God, no! I can't believe this."

I wanted to stab a silver crucifix through that motherfucking nun's black, rosary bead–sized heart.

"I felt so terrible, Mom," Harry said, his voice cracking, "I was on the verge of tears when she said, 'There are *some* homosexuals who don't practice.' Then she asked me why I wasn't seeking professional help."

"What? Is she crazy? How dare she talk to you that way!"

"I told her I didn't need help because I didn't have a *problem*. By that time I felt tears on my cheeks, and she asked me why I was crying. When I told her this was a situation I'd wanted to avoid, she said, 'If you don't want to cry anymore, stop talking. Silence. Be silent.' I was just so shocked, Mom, and I felt like she was threatening me."

I wiped away a rivulet of my own and realized this was the first time that a person in authority had not only not stood up for Harry, she had attacked him. I flashed back to the year I was Harry's age and my mother had chased me around the kitchen table swinging a leather dog leash.

"Oh, Harry," I choked, "I am so sorry you had to go through this. That woman is a monster. She had no right talking to you that way. I wish I could be there with you right now."

Harry felt so far away he might as well have been in outer space. I had to take over from Earth Central Control. I clicked into Mom 911 mode.

"What about your Spanish mom? Does she know about this?"

"No, I came right home from school and called you."

"You have to tell her, Harry. She has to know. You can't stay at that school."

"Ugh," he groaned. "I don't even want to go back there tomorrow."

"Harry, I'm not going to say you have to, but if you don't go you're giving up your power to that Mother Superior, and she deserves no power. It's up to you. Either way, somehow we're going to get you transferred to that public school they said was full. I swear, Harry, something good will come of this."

After we hung up, I felt numb. Harry had been mortified. This was not the worldly experience promised in the AFS brochure. I called Ken's direct line at the studio and told him the whole story.

"This is unbelievable," Ken groaned. "That poor kid."

"I want him to come home, Ken. Will you back me on that?"

"Can we do that? Will Harry do that?"

"I don't know," I said, "But I'll figure it out. Enough is enough, right?"

"Yeah, I think it's time," Ken agreed.

I opened the kitchen desk drawer and pulled out the Shorewood High School Directory. I made an appointment with Harry's guidance counselor. I couldn't imagine the situation in Spain getting any worse, and I needed to know that Harry could return for second semester without any problems.

When I got a call two days later from Courtney at AFS National, I realized that instead of going to the high school to meet with Harry's counselor, I should be seeing my doctor for some anti-anxiety medication. I learned that at the same time Harry had been telling me about his visit to the Mother Superior's office, her Supreme Evilness had called Harry's mom in Spain to complain about him and blamed her for allowing a homosexual into her school.

Courtney assured me Harry's mom cared about him and thought he was a great kid, but she felt so pressured by the town's church officials that she just couldn't keep Harry anymore. It was a small town, she'd said, and people were talking. AFS Madrid was going to have to find Harry another family.

I was completely stunned. "Do you realize what you're putting Harry through?"

I thought of him having to face another episode of rejection, this time from Spanish parents he felt comfortable with, and I wanted to throw up.

"You have to let me tell him," I said. "I don't want him to hear this from anyone else."

"All right," Courtney said. "I can arrange that. But Friday will have to be his last day. There's a midsemester weekend retreat in Madrid for all AFS students. Tell Harry to bring all of his things with him."

I went up to Harry's room, sat down on his bed and broke down in loud wails. The thought of telling him he was going to have to switch families and schools for the fifth time felt like theater of the absurd. This couldn't be going more wrong. I searched for the words that would let him down in the gentlest way. I would tell him the truth: that his Spanish parents just didn't have the resources to deal with the outrageous bullying behavior of a vicious Mother Superior and her church henchmen. I picked up the blue stuffed toy bear Harry left propped against his pillow and held it to my face, hopeful I could breathe in some of his strength. I knew he'd want to stick it out in Spain for the remainder of the school year, but I was going to tell him one semester was enough. It was time to come home.

He called me Saturday morning from the student orientation in Madrid, sounding like his happy, confident self.

"Mom, you're not going to believe what happened on my last day at school!" he exclaimed. "It was amaaaazing!"

"What? Tell me!" I couldn't wait to hear some good news for a change.

"Well, I wasn't going to tell anyone it was my last day, because I didn't want to have to deal with explaining anything, but I did tell my math teacher before class, because she was cool and I liked her."

"Was she a nun?"

"No, she wasn't. But at the end of class she tells everyone to be sure and say goodbye to me, because it's my last day. In the courtyard afterwards some friends wanted to know why I was leaving, so I told them what happened with the Mother Superior. All of a sudden they start chanting in Spanish, 'Tolerance! Tolerance! Out with the nuns!' And then the whole student body joined in."

I covered my mouth as chills shot through me. I pictured Harry standing in the middle of a crowd chanting over and over in support of him.

"Oh, Harry! That sounds incredible!"

"It was! And none of the teachers could quiet them down. So the Mother Superior came out. She clapped her hands and the kids stopped. Then she said, 'I only called Harry into my office the other day to help him. Isn't that right, Harry?' And I could not believe she was saying that. So I said, 'No, you're a liar. And a witch!'"

"What?" I said, laughing. "You really said that to her face?"

"I did! All of the kids started cheering and they wouldn't stop. It felt so good!"

"Oh, Harry, what a great ending!"

"Yeah, it is pretty great, isn't it?"

After our call, I felt like I'd just finished watching an *ABC After-school Special.* I could see the description in the TV guide: "A gay teenager studying abroad stands up to the homophobic Mother Superior at a Catholic school while the whole student body cheers him on." Harry had just made my day the happiest in months. I couldn't wait to tell everyone.

Harry spent the next ten days in a youth hostel in Madrid along with three other kids who'd also left their Spanish families. According to Harry, they all had horror stories. One girl hadn't been allowed to leave the house and was expected to teach their son English. Another girl said she'd repeatedly caught the father at her second family watching her sleep. And a third girl's family would only speak to her in English. Background checks, my ass, I thought. I wasn't crazy about the idea of Harry running loose in Madrid when he should have been in school, but at least he was out of the clutches of the Dark Ages.

After calling everyone I could think of with contacts in Europe, a friend of my sister knew of a family in northwestern Spain who would take Harry in and register him for school those remaining five weeks of the semester. I couldn't wait to get him back home.

Ken and I met Harry at the Milwaukee airport five days before Christmas. His Aunt Jean was there with a sign decorated with curly red ribbon and a pinecone ornament that read, "Bien Venido Casa Harry!" Ian, Kayla, and three other friends of Harry's from school skipped out of the last day of class and took the bus there to greet him with a welcome-back sign and some little cakes.

I stood with my camera as close to the security gate on Concourse D as was allowed. "He's here!" I yelled with a little jump when I saw him.

He was wearing the navy parka with a bright orange and yellow stripe he'd asked me to send him. A white scarf with a Middle Eastern print was wrapped around his neck. He wasn't wearing his glasses, and long bangs covered his eyes. I noticed his gait was different; it was slower, more confident. He appeared older than he did when we'd said goodbye to him at JFK three and a half months earlier. I couldn't wait to hug him, the boy who had smacked down the Catholic Church in Spain and survived triumphant.

As Harry neared me, I realized how amazed I was by the fortitude of this kid. I had felt so helplessly out of control when I couldn't be there to protect him from ignorance and persecution, yet he had managed to stand up for himself with conviction. He hadn't cowered. He hadn't pretended to be something he wasn't. And he was only fifteen years old. I had always loved Harry for just being Harry, and I'd believed in him. And now this remarkable teenager was doing those things for himself. I was bursting with pride, or as his Great-Aunt Anita would say, I was "kvelling." And more than that, I marveled at Harry's ability to never forget who he was.

High school graduation, class of 2008

Ken Hanson

The Graduation Stilettos

Where're you headed?" our cabbie asked Harry, who then glanced at me.

Annoyed, I shook my head. Even though Harry was two months shy of his eighteenth birthday, cab drivers in Las Vegas continued to direct their questions to him, not me. It was the same in restaurants, where waiters set the check down in front of Harry. I felt like I was traveling with Rusty Griswold, Chevy Chase's under-age son from the '90s flick *Vegas Vacation*, who rode around town with an entourage of older women and who casino staff believed was high-roller wunderkind Mr. Papagiorgio. But this was 2008. Could these men really think a teenager was my escort?

"We're going to Lucky Cheng's Restaurant," I said.

Our driver hesitated. "So you're in the mood for a little Chinese food, huh?"

"No," I replied. "It's a dinner-theater drag show."

"Oh, I know that," he said, looking at me in the rearview mirror.

"Just wanted to make sure you did. Some people go expecting egg rolls and chow mein."

I had no idea what the drag club would be like, but I wasn't the clueless middle-aged tourist our driver thought I was. I was excited to see the show Harry had chosen for the night and felt flattered he was bringing me into his world of drag performance. I'd told him in November that I wanted to take him to Las Vegas over Martin Luther King Jr. weekend as an early birthday present. My plan was to wow him with Cirque du Soleil's aquatic show *O*, the new musical *Beatles LOVE*, and a pyrotechnic version of *Phantom of the Opera*, which he'd never seen. I'd figured that if we went to the Sunday matinee of *LOVE*, we could squeeze in something else that night. I wanted to let Harry pick the fourth show and rattled off a list of other entertainment options to him over the phone one night when he was at Ken's.

"You know, Mom, I'd kind of like to see a drag show."

My eyes blinked in rapid succession. "A drag show?"

"Yeah, I've never been to one."

Of course Harry would be eager to see professional drag queens in action. *The Rocky Horror Picture Show* was still his favorite extracurricular. He had joined the local cast as soon as he was legally able to, shoving a parental permission form in front of me the day after his sixteenth birthday. Now, almost two years later, he performed the role of Trixie, the sassy hostess that entertained *Rocky* fans waiting in line outside. His elaborate wardrobe and extensive wig collection transformed him semimonthly from high school senior to flamboyant caricatures of Marie Antoinette or Jessica Rabbit. He never wore the same look twice.

"I haven't seen a drag show either, honey, so why not? I'm searching Google right now."

"Awesome, Mom, thanks."

"Let's see. The Flamingo headlines female impersonators. There's a Cher, Madonna, Tina Turner, Liza Minelli, and other celebrities. A Joan Rivers hosts. The Flamingo's a hotel, so that'll be a big floor show."

"Is that the only one?"

"There's a Lucky Cheng's Restaurant I've never heard of," I said clicking to the site. "It says, 'Drag performers sing live, lip-sync and dance throughout the dining room . . . audience participation . . . irreverent sense of humor—'"

"Definitely that one, Mom!"

"They do have a Sunday night show, so consider us booked."

The cab dropped us off in front of a darkened venue. There was no sign and the place looked closed. We stepped into a dim entryway. Three sets of stackable dining chairs stood to our right next to two fake wood laminate tables, one inverted on top of the other. Some sound equipment and cords were shoved under a long table to the left. I was wondering if we were in the right place when a very attractive woman in a strapless silver-sequined dress pushed aside a black curtain.

"Welcome to Lucky Cheng's," she smiled. "I'm Asia." Her voice was hoarse and deep; it was the only giveaway that she was a drag queen. She towered over me atop clear, Cinderella-slipper stilettos. I marveled at her supermodel-perfect hair and makeup.

"Follow me, please," she said.

As Harry whispered that her dress was really two tube tops,

Asia stopped at the edge of the dining room. "Short bitch walking and her fag," she yelled.

Everyone laughed. I felt all of my body heat rush to my face. Harry turned to look at me with a huge grin, signing with rapid head bobs that this was going to be fun.

During the preshow dinner, Asia picked up the bangle handle of my patchwork snakeskin wristlet. "Look at this!" she said to Bebe, another glam waitress and the current Miss Pride Las Vegas. "Cher here's got a cock ring on her purse!"

Harry laughed while I managed a smirk, stiffening like an over-sprayed wig.

"Who made that thing, anyway?" Bebe asked. "Jeffrey Dahmer?"

Harry was having a blast. I felt like a prude. I knew if I were with my girlfriends I'd be lapping up the funny insults and references to huge dicks, too. But I was with my son. I wanted to maintain some parental decorum. I ordered a vodka martini straight up.

During the stage show, Harry and I tipped all the queens from the stack of singles we'd been encouraged to get from the bar in advance. Harry shared critiques of the performers with me between acts.

"She looks tired and bored," Harry said of Miss Fortune, the emcee. "And she put no effort at all into her makeup."

He was right. She didn't look half as good as Harry did when he'd hosted the Miss Shorewood High Drag Pageant as Christina Draguliera the year before. His glittered eye makeup had resembled peacock feathers, and the sleek purple-sequined gown was an outfit I'd envisioned Marlene Dietrich wearing. I'd been apprehensive about him taking his tiara-topped femme fatale look to the high school campus. Even though the pageant had been his brainchild as a fundraiser for the student council's charity, the Shorewood High School auditorium at seven o'clock was a time warp away from the Oriental Theatre at midnight.

The drag pageant's tonight and you haven't rehearsed?" I'd asked nervously as he'd rushed down the stairs carrying a box overflowing with blond wigs, feather boas, and gold lamé. Before he had time to answer, I flashed on the audience. "What about the jocks and football players, honey? Have you thought about how they're going to react?"

"Don't worry, Mom," Harry replied. "They're in it."

"They are?"

"Yeah, I recruited 'em. It's for charity. And, besides, straight guys actually like dressing up in women's clothes."

While Flip Wilson and Benny Hill paraded through my mind, Harry brushed a kiss on my cheek.

"I gotta go, Ian's waiting in the car. See you there?"

"Of course! I wouldn't miss it, honey."

Harry's poster for the pageant, promising "real drag queens, real prizes, and lots of fake hair!" was taped to the exterior door of the auditorium when I arrived. The photo of him in full regalia spared no detail, right down to press-on nails. Inside the theater I did a double take; hundreds of people were already seated. In addition to students, I saw other parents, faculty, and administrators. I took an aisle seat in the center orchestra and then looked around. Ian's mom sat a few rows up. She turned to wave and then gave me a thumbs-up. Fidgeting, I couldn't believe Harry was going to wing it in front of a packed house. A part of me stressed that Harry was going to shock people. This wasn't some club in San Francisco; it was a suburban high school.

The audience applauded the moment my glitterati son walked out on stage, and the laughs began with his humorous welcome to a pageant unlike any other in Shorewood. The jocks in miniskirts tripping in their heels were hilarious. And everyone roared at Harry's banter with the contestants, including his onstage questions for the finalists during the pageant interview. I clapped, too, realizing how silly I'd been to worry. Of course, people knew who Harry was. He was now just working the stage as an entertainer. He was as comfortable in the spotlight as he was in sequins, and the whole audience had jumped on his drag pageant train. I was proud of him for being himself, for having so much talent, and for putting on a show that raised nine hundred dollars for an orphanage in Guatemala. Harry was a superstar.

As I watched the low-energy Miss Fortune at Lucky Cheng's, I thought Harry would have done a much better job as emcee. Just then she asked for audience volunteers to participate in a contest. Harry's hand shot up, so I watched as he and five others took to the stage. They were to perform their best imitation of Meg Ryan's fake orgasm from the movie, *When Harry Met Sally*. Audience applause would determine the winner.

I gulped as my heart moved up into my throat. I had to listen to my teenage son fake an orgasm? I'd never even said "orgasm" in front of him. But Harry was in his element: center stage. I knew my natural-born performer was going to give it his all. My lips curved to a frozen smile. I took a deep breath and imagined myself invisible.

Harry's fake orgasm was one of the best, but I could not focus my senses fully on the applause meter. Sound echoed in my head. I was sure the metallic sensation in my mouth was the taste of extreme embarrassment. I sat with ankles crossed and clapped like a white-gloved monarch, three fingers of my left hand gently tapping the heel of my right hand.

"Hey!" Miss Fortune shouted, pointing at me. "You're with him and you're not even clapping!"

I felt my face turn the shade of the brick I'd just been hit with. I changed my applause on cue and even shouted a few woo-hoos.

Harry took second place. I thanked my lucky stars I didn't have to watch him down the prize of a Slippery Nipple shooter.

"You did great, honey," I told him when he returned to the table. "I almost fainted, but you were awesome."

"Thanks, Mom," Harry whispered. "I wasn't sure, because I never saw that movie."

Oh my God, are you kidding me? "Well, no one would have known that, I assure you."

After the show I slid my credit card across the table to Harry. "Here, this is for Asia when she brings the check. I have to use the restroom."

When I returned, most of the guests were milling around chatting. Harry stood a few feet from our table talking to Bebe. I saw her slip him a folded note. Was Miss Pride Las Vegas hitting on my son? I took my seat and Harry joined me.

"Here, Mom, you need to sign this," he said, pushing over the plastic tray that held my credit card and a pen.

"What did Bebe have to say?" I asked, clicking the top of the ballpoint.

"Oh, we just exchanged email addresses," he replied. "So, when Asia brought back your credit card, I told her it was my mother's and that you would sign when you got back. Then the guy sitting behind me turned around, and said, 'That's your *mother?*'"

I forced a smile. Harry knew I liked hearing that someone didn't believe I was his mother. But I still felt unnerved when it happened in Las Vegas.

"I said yes," Harry continued. "And then he asked if you knew I was gay. I told him I came out when I was fourteen. He said I was lucky, because when he told his mom after college, the only thing she'd said was, 'Do we have to tell anyone?'"

I looked at the man standing at his chair behind Harry, laughing with his group of friends. I wondered if his mother ever had accepted him for who he was, or if he tried not to think about that aspect of their relationship.

"That makes me sad and angry at the same time," I said. "I want to hug that man and tell him I'll be his mother."

"Well, he's right, Mom. I am lucky."

"No, honey," I smiled. "I'm the lucky one."

I pushed away from the table, slipped my cock ring onto my wrist and put an arm around Harry. "Come on, honey. Let's head back."

"You know, Mom, I think I'm gonna go out for a while on my own."

"Really? We have such an early flight tomorrow morning."

"I know, but it's really not that late. I've got my camera and feel like taking some pictures. All the lights here make it daylight even at night."

I didn't like the idea of Harry wondering around Sin City, but I couldn't argue. He had proven in Madrid he could navigate a city where clubs stayed open all night. Plus, photography was his art, and Las Vegas was a jackpot of subject matter.

"All right, but please get back to the hotel at a decent time." I said, rubbing his back. "Bubble of light, Harry, bubble of light."

Harry nodded. I'd been telling him that before going out at night for the past four months. That's how much time had passed since he'd been mugged two blocks from his dad's house on his way home from a gender-bender party. His call had woken me at eleven o'clock on a Sunday night.

What do you mean gender-bender?" I'd asked, after learning he wasn't harmed.

"You know, a mix-it-up party. My beard is half-shaved off."

I switched on the light. "What happened?"

"I was on my bike when all of a sudden three teenagers rode up and forced me off the road. One of them pulled out a knife. He said he'd cut me if I didn't give him my phone."

I knew Harry was okay, but I still felt short of breath as I imagined him surrounded in the dark facing a weapon. "Oh, Harry, you must have been so scared. I hope you gave it to him."

"I did."

"Good!"

"Then he wanted my wallet, and I said I didn't have any money."

"You didn't?"

"No, I did. My wallet was at the bottom of my backpack, but I wasn't going to give it to him," Harry said with belligerence.

"Jesus, Harry, you have to give up your wallet!"

"Then they wanted to know what was in my backpack. When I pulled out one of my red patent leather knee-high platforms, the guy said, 'Hey, what are you? Are you a faggot? Wanna suck my dick, faggot? Wanna suck my dick?'"

A chill swept the back of my neck.

"I told them it was my girlfriend's. Then a car turned the corner onto Kenilworth. That's when he pushed me and my bike onto the street, and they sped off."

"Oh my God, Harry," I said, trembling. "Is your dad home? Did you call the police?"

"Dad's out, but I talked to him, and he said to call the police. That was a couple of hours ago. They came here to fill out a report and then made me drive around with them looking for the guys. They just left. Can you get a copy of the phone records sent to the detective's email?"

"Yes, of course. Are you sure you're okay? Do you want me to come over there?"

"No, Mom, I'm fine. A few scrapes and a little shaken up is all."

Ever since that happened I imagined Harry being safe in the universe, protected by a bubble of light, the same bubble that Glinda had traveled in.

As we walked out of Lucky Cheng's, Harry adjusted his camera strap with the button "Eat! Fuck! Kill!" pinned on it. "Don't worry, Mom. I'll be fine."

Bubble of light.

I had to face facts though. That protective bubble of light wasn't going to keep me from becoming an empty nester in the fall. And while I was preparing psychologically for living alone while Harry was a thousand miles away, I didn't want my world without him to define me. Rather than anticipate the loneliness of daily life without Harry, I was set on being open to positive change and other possibilities.

I reached for the book I'd brought from home and set on the nightstand, *The Nature of Personality Reality: Specific, Practical Techniques for Solving Everyday Problems and Enriching the Life You Know*, a Seth book by Jane Roberts. Seth was a highly respected spiritual teacher, considered by many to have launched the New Age movement in the '70s. I'd just discovered the book that fall and felt the need to read it while holding a yellow highlighter. The book was based on Seth's philosophy that we create our own reality through our thoughts and emotions. The material was helping me worry less about the past or the present. I was working on the exercise that suggested I examine my beliefs and identify those I thought were limiting me. I knew I had feared becoming my mother as a parent and had also believed from childhood that I was an unlovable person. I learned that just because I believed something didn't mean it was true. I was beginning to trust myself and trust the world more. I practiced expecting things to turn out the way I wanted them to be.

I closed the book at midnight and dialed the hotel switchboard for a 6:30 a.m. wake-up call. I felt a nanosecond surge of panic as I wondered what Harry was doing. But I didn't want to think about the worst that could happen. I reminded myself that Harry was smart, aware, and in the bubble. Then I remembered the note Bebe had given him. I told myself he was with her. I imagined them dancing under a disco ball. Or maybe they were exchanging hair and makeup tips.

I woke to the sound of Harry unlocking our hotel room door. I checked my phone. It was five-thirty in the morning. He would get only two hours of sleep, but he was safe, just as I had assured myself he would be. I closed my eyes.

Back home, I was glad I'd planned our Las Vegas trip before the start of second semester. Harry ended up spending his spring break in New York visiting friends at New York University, one of the schools where he'd been accepted. While he was gone, I flew to Colorado to ski with friends and met Jeff, an expert skier and business consultant from Denver. Our chairlift rides and discussions about beliefs shaping reality led to a couple of dinners where the exchange of ideas continued. He reminded me of Chris Agyris's ladder of inference in Peter M. Senge's *The Fifth Discipline: The Art and Practice of the Learning Organization*, which explained how we jump to conclusions based on our beliefs. Jeff recommended a research piece on measurable psychological capacities from one of his trade publications. I had to buy the article in order to download it when I got home. Then I applied the paper's thinking about the qualities of effective leaders to my feng shui business that was morphing into a personal leadership development practice. And I recognized that the positive characteristics researcher Fred Luthans described as psychological capital—confidence, hope, optimism, and resilience—were all attributes I'd used to describe Harry. There was no doubt my son was born the strong, determined leader of himself. I'd been resilient as a kid, refusing to be broken by my parents' ideas on childrearing. But I'd had to learn the other three traits.

At the beginning of April, Harry received an acceptance letter from Wesleyan University in Connecticut and told me that was where he wanted to go.

"But what about NYU film school?" I asked, incredulous he would pass that up.

"I decided I want more of a campus life for undergrad," he said. "I can go there for graduate school."

"I'm sorry, Harry, but I'm not sending you anywhere you haven't visited first. What if you don't like it there?"

"But we're in the middle of rehearsals for *Beauty and the Beast*! Dreesen will never let me off so close to opening night."

"Listen, Harry, I'm sure she can spare Cogsworth for a couple of days. I'm calling Alice, who lives in Brooklyn now. We can stay with her and take the train up to Wesleyan. We're doing this."

I marveled how at every turn Harry remained so confident in his choices and the vision he had for his life. I would have been too afraid at his age to commit to four years somewhere without having experienced it first. But Harry was the kind of person who could decide on a college sight unseen because he just knew it was what he wanted. I felt inspired to take charge of my soon-to-be-solo life, express my own independence, and find new challenges.

I'd never been to Brooklyn. But I felt instantly at home among the tree-lined blocks of brownstones, shops, and restaurants. Alice's

Boerum Hill neighborhood reminded me of Wrigleyville in Chicago. There was comfort in this borough's midwestern vibe.

"You know, I didn't think I could ever live in Manhattan," I told Alice as we passed a joint in the backyard garden of her townhouse. "But I could really see myself in Brooklyn."

"Julie!" Alice gasped. "You *must* move here. I insist. Think of how much fun we'd have!"

"That goes without saying," I laughed. "I'm going to downsize to a condo after Harry goes to college in the fall, but none of the places I've looked at feel right to me. Maybe that's because I'm supposed to move to Brooklyn."

The backyard breeze was warm, but I felt cold shivers on my arms and a tingling in my shoulders at the thought of uprooting myself so completely. Before meeting Ken, I'd always pictured myself on one of the coasts. I worked with clients by phone, so location didn't matter. Harry was certainly a big city kid. I couldn't imagine him moving back to Milwaukee after college and thought he already had designs on living in New York City.

On our train ride back to Alice's from Wesleyan, I pictured a Brooklyn brownstone flat with dark wood floors and a balcony, close to Alice and the Brooklyn Academy of Music or Prospect Park. I giggled to myself and felt light-headed. I had just given myself permission to do something daring and different. I could take a risk and it wouldn't matter what anybody else thought. Then I looked at Harry. I cared what he thought. I tapped him on the arm, and he took out his ear buds.

"Harry," I said, leaning forward. "I'm thinking of moving to New York after you leave for college."

"Really?" he asked, his eyes wide.

"Yeah, but I want to make sure it won't seem like I'm stalking you if I move out here."

"Mom, I'll be in Connecticut. It's not even the same state."

"But what about after, if you're in New York?"

"It's a big city, Mom. It will be fine if you're here."

"Are you sure?"

"Yes, I'm excited for you! Plus I want to get summer jobs in New York, so now I can live with you during my internships."

"Yea!" I said, smiling so hard that my cheeks hurt. That was it. I was going to become a New Yorker.

During Harry's last weeks of high school, while fantasizing about selling my home in Milwaukee and finding an apartment in Brooklyn, I made lists of everything I had to do to send him off to college. There was a dorm refrigerator to order, meal plans to choose, and health insurance waivers to sign. A few days before graduation, Harry came home with his red cap and gown.

"I think I'm going to wear my red platform stilettos with this outfit," he said, holding up the full-length red garment in front of himself.

"Harry, you can't wear heels to your high school graduation!"

"Why not? I wear them with all of my other gowns."

I shook my head with disapproval. "Please think it over, Harry. Graduation is a serious ceremony."

"There's nothing to think about, Mom. I'm wearing them."

I remembered the night two years earlier when Harry had worn black patent leather pumps with jeans and a military-styled jacket I'd bought on Melrose Place in Los Angeles in the '80s out on the auditorium stage to introduce the "Trashy Fashion" line he'd put together for the high school's Talent Showcase. The drama teacher Ms. Dreesen had shared my trepidation about Harry wearing heels out on stage.

"Why not?" Harry told me backstage, "Galliano wears them."

"Who's that?" I asked.

"He's the fashion director at Christian Dior, Mom."

Of course, he knew that, and I didn't. The kids in the audience that night had cheered and whooped for Harry the moment he walked out from behind the curtain.

On the night of graduation, Harry and I met Ken and my Aunt Margie at Carini's Italian restaurant near the high school. Harry was wearing a white tuxedo shirt, black-and-white glen plaid pants, a red tie, and his black Converse sneakers. I could only hope that he'd changed his mind about the red stilettos. It just didn't seem right for a commencement ceremony. After parking in the Shorewood High lot, Harry grabbed his Chrome messenger bag and ran into the auditorium to change. When he came back outside dressed in his red satin gown and mortarboard, he was still in sneakers. I took pictures of him and his friends, and Aunt Margie took a shot of Harry with Ken and me. It had been drizzling earlier, and the light was perfect for photos of beaming teenagers all in red.

Ken and I took our seats in the auditorium. When Harry's name was called, Ken lifted his camera, and we watched our son sashay in high heels across the auditorium like it was a runway during Fashion Week. The front rows filled with students clapped, hooted, and pounded their feet as Harry accepted his diploma. He turned to wave as he walked off, and by then applause had ignited across the room and up into the balcony.

I was misty eyed and my hands stung from clapping. Ken's eyes were wet, too, and we exchanged the jubilant look of proud parents.

"A mind of his own," Ken whispered in my ear.

"That's for damn sure," I said.

Ken was referring to the birth announcement he'd designed for Harry. Under date, time, weight, and height, Ken had added the line of copy, "Already has a mind of his own." Truer words about a personality had never been predicted. Harry was unabashedly Harry.

Ken Hanson

Christmas dinner in Milwaukee, 2011

The Glass Half Full

The narrow full-length mirror that had moved with me to Brooklyn eight months earlier leaned against the wall of my walk-in closet atop a short stack of boot boxes next to my printer. I smoothed a long black tee over my new dark denim cigarette jeans, but my reflection stopped at my calves. I made a mental note to search the Brooklyn Flea for a distressed antique floor mirror for the still-blank wall in my bedroom. I picked out the new pink peep-toe Melissa flats from my favorite neighborhood boutique, where a white piglet-sized French bulldog named Bianca always greeted me.

I set my shoes down at the front door and walked barefoot over to the glass table that now served as both my desk and dining room table. I closed the lid on my laptop and straightened a client's set of blueprints. It was only one o'clock in the afternoon, but my work could wait. One of my favorite singers, Sharon Jones, was making an in-studio appearance on WNYC's show *Soundcheck*. I'd made up my mind before moving to New York to start saying "yes" to myself and doing what I wanted to do. I had decided it was time to give myself the same approval and options I'd tried to give Harry.

I looked up from my dining table–desk and scanned the open floor plan of my Brooklyn apartment. A panoramic smile spread across my face. The knock-off Barcelona chairs, Alice's six-foot paintings, and my grandmother's Limoges plates that were now my everyday dishes were all in view because I'd chosen them to be there. Unlike my closet mirror, they were a complete reflection of me in my New York City life. I'd pared down my belongings to only the things I loved. I was focused on letting myself go and being more spontaneous. This was my new stance. I said "yes" to myself and expected the best outcome from every situation. I gave myself a mental hug, grabbed my clutch, slipped on my flats, and headed out for the subway.

The sun warmed my face as I walked along the uneven slabs of slate that formed the sidewalks in my historic Prospect Heights neighborhood. I paused in front of a tall blooming lilac shrub at the iron gate of a neighbor's fence. Standing on tiptoes, I pulled down a low-hanging branch and pressed the short lavender spear to my nose. I was sure I looked ridiculous standing there with my face in the flowers, but I didn't care what anyone thought. The fresh, not-too-sweet fragrance filled my nostrils. One block up I stopped in the middle of the sidewalk and breathed "wow." A fluffy layer of cherry blossoms covered the street corner like pink confetti. Invigorated by the beauty, I pulled out my cell phone and sent a text image to Harry at college with the message, "NYC snow, April 2010." I decided flowering trees would be my new marker for springtime.

That weekend I got a call from my Londoner friend Camille, one of the fun women I'd hung out with after Ken and I'd split up. She'd moved to Aspen a couple of weeks after Harry left for Spain.

"Jules!" she exclaimed. "How the hell are you?"

"Honestly, Cam, I feel like I'm on permanent vacation."

"Aw, that's so great. What have you been up to?"

"Well, for starters I joined all the art museums, the Brooklyn Botanical Gardens, and the Prospect Park Alliance. The Brooklyn Museum had an amazing photography show on the history of rock and roll. And, get this, Blondie played at the opening reception!"

"That's New York for you."

"I know, right? I go to as much theater as I can afford, too. Harry and I saw Cate Blanchett in *A Streetcar Named Desire* at Brooklyn Academy of Music over his Thanksgiving break."

"Harry," Camille said wistfully. "How is that boy?"

"He's great, as always. Loves school. I saw him in Milwaukee over Christmas. We both stayed at Ken and Katharine's."

"I still don't know how you and Ken do it."

"That's what everyone says. I think we'll always be close friends. Katharine calls me her sister wife. We watch HBO's *Big Love* together."

"Hey, have you seen James lately?" she asked.

"We met for a burger in the West Village right after he moved here. He's working on his app start-up. But he's living with two chain smokers, so he takes his laptop to a coffee shop every day. He seems a little stressed. I try to be encouraging."

Camille laughed.

"Why is that so funny?"

"Because I talked to him after that, and he said you were just so positive about everything all the time now. He said it was a little sickening."

"What? He said 'sickening'?"

"Oh, you know how comedic James is. The way he said it was just funny."

I thought James was one of the most naturally humorous people I knew. He reminded me of Jerry Seinfeld. I was a little hurt he hadn't made fun of me to my face.

"Well, I'm going to have to tell him it's okay to tease me about my New York outlook. The next time I text him I'll remember to sign it 'Pollyanna.'"

Lying in bed later, I thought about what James had told Camille.

It wasn't as simple as just being positive. I'd been doing a lot of hard personal work. I'd recognized that I'd spent much of my life with feelings of unworthiness and powerlessness I didn't know how to handle. I'd started attending Seth classes twice a month with Rick Stack, who had been a student in Jane Roberts's ESP classes in the early '70s. I paid attention to how I felt during the day. Then I tried to figure out the thought that had led to the feeling, especially any negative ones. If we were all energy beings, why couldn't we control our own energy to create the experiences we wanted? I had seen the evidence of that theory in my own life and had begun to test it with good results in my consultation work, too. It seemed more than a coincidence that the title of the first section of Senge's book *The Fifth Discipline* echoed Seth's idea that our actions create our reality and that we can change it. Action was merely thought in motion. I was carrying that outlook out into the world with me. I wanted to be guided by positive expectation, not fear. I had spent so much time over the years concerned about Harry, and it never did any good. I didn't want to waste my time on worry anymore.

Later that spring I took the train to Manhattan to catch a friend's after-work jazz concert in Bryant Park. In the subway car I smiled at an ad that read, "You didn't move to NYC to stay home." The teenager next to me playing a game on his smartphone and the woman reading a script with lips moving didn't hear my audible sigh of happiness.

I arrived early, so I strolled up Fifth Avenue. I sat down on a bench in Rockefeller Plaza next to a large raised garden of red and yellow tulips. I checked my email and settled in for some people watching. A man was taking a photo of his family in front of the fountain. I offered to take a picture of all of them. I felt giddy being a New Yorker who could give tourists a fun memory.

My fondness for shoes soon drew me to the sale across the street at Sak's. After two decades of focusing on my son's love of shoes, I was now concentrating on what looked good on my own feet. I browsed the shopper-crowded racks of eye-candy footwear. I didn't want to buy something just because it was on sale. Then I picked up a black satin open-toed Kate Spade heel with a rhinestone clasp at the ankle strap. It was perfect for two shoeless dresses hanging in my closet. But it was size eleven, too big for me.

"Excuse me," I said to a sales associate. "Do you have these in a six and a half?"

"All we have is what's on the floor," he said in a monotone.

"Well, if you wouldn't mind checking another store . . ."

After punching the computer keyboard a few times, he told me there was one store with two pairs in my size.

"Yes!" I exclaimed.

"Just because the computer shows they're there, doesn't mean they are," he warned. "Our computer inventory isn't always up to date."

"Well, I'm going to think only positively that there's still one pair left for me."

His stance relaxed and his face softened. "Yes, you're right," he said. "I need to be more positive. Thank you for bringing me back to where I want to be."

"The pleasure is all mine," I said. I felt quite satisfied that a pair of exquisite heels was on its way to me. I couldn't wait to show them to Harry. He had landed a summer internship working for the fashion director at *Cosmopolitan* magazine. I was excited about seeing him and had been busy transforming my guest room into Harry's room. His childhood teddy bear Brambles sat on a wall shelf I'd added above the TV stand.

"I don't separate summer or winter clothes, Mom," Harry told me when six huge boxes arrived via UPS. "Except for coats, I wear all my clothes all year."

"Even so, Harry, how much stuff did you bring?"

"Two boxes are shoes," he said, defending the shipment. "I want to start checking out the performance scene in Brooklyn, and I didn't have a lot of my drag wardrobe at school." Then in the tone that belonged to his drag persona Amber Alert, he added, "So I've been doin' a little shoppin' at Savers."

"What's Savers?"

"It's like the East Coast Value Village, a little more expensive but still some great deals." His eyes lit up and he grinned wider than a dress hanger. "Wait until you see the lavender jumpsuit I found!"

"I can't wait for a show-and-tell, honey," I said. "I've got some things to show you, too."

"By the way, Mom, have you found a good tailor?" he asked. "I bought a gown with some loose beads that need tacking down at the shoulders and hem."

"Yes. There's a guy at my drycleaners on Flatbush who's very detailed. Just show me what you want done and I can drop it off next time I'm there."

Before Memorial Day weekend, I left the apartment with Harry's vintage beaded gown draped over my arm in clear plastic. On my way to the tailor, I ran into a neighbor whose mother was visiting from California.

"That's some dress you've got there," she said.

"Oh, this belongs to my son," I replied. "I told him I'd take it in for a little repair. He's a drag queen who always has great luck at thrift stores." As soon as the words "drag queen" tumbled from my mouth, I realized how gratifying it was to say them. Harry was living the authentic self he'd known since childhood, and rather than worry about reactions I could finally just celebrate him.

"Really?" she asked.

It was the same "Really?" I'd heard from other women in New York who recognized my luck at having a queer man into fashion for a son. Those who knew it meant I had my own free personal stylist.

In July, my friend Eve from Sacramento moved to Brooklyn. We'd met in Miami in 2003 attending private feng shui graduate courses. Eve had begun reading the Seth books, too. We also shared interests in quantum physics and the role of energy at the subatomic level, as well as the field of neuroscience, specifically the study of positivity and how the brain handles emotions.

We joined a Meetup group called the Brainiacs and over the next year attended roundtables where heavy hitters in physics, math, and philosophy discussed topics like "The Limitations of Mental and Physical Reality" and "Theories of Everything" at the Philoctetes Center in New York City. We saw the brain exhibit at the Museum of Natural History and went to presentations put on by the Secret Science Club in Brooklyn. In June 2011 we got tickets for a night at the 4th Annual World Science Festival where a Nobel Prize–winning physicist joined other noted scientists for a discussion of their theory that the universe was a hologram.

I inched forward on my lecture hall chair, practically falling off as I listened to those leaders in physics challenge the paradigm of how we typically viewed the world. My body buzzed as if I'd had eight shots of espresso in my tall skinny latte. Their beliefs that our reality was a projection and that there was a possible pre-quantum world of information seemed entirely possible. I wanted to take control of my inner information and shape my own reality. It was my intent to create joyful realities wherever I went.

Harry's internship that summer was as studio manager for a portrait photographer in Manhattan, but I hardly ever saw him. He worked long hours and went out with friends at night. I worked on the website for my personal leadership consulting business and continued to take full advantage of all the culture New York had to offer. The two of us managed to find a date at the end of July to see the Alexander McQueen fashion exhibition at the Metropolitan Museum.

Harry came out of his room that morning wearing a long plaid skirt, a black button-up chiffon shirt, and a black mesh beach coverup that hung over both. On his feet were the black "Lolita" lace-up platforms I'd ordered for him from China the previous

Christmas. His hair was on top of his head in a tight knot, exposing the back undercut. I was impressed at how he always knew how to put together a look.

"Are you sure that's what you want to wear, honey?" I asked. And for the first time in my life I wasn't asking because it was a skirt. I was questioning his fabric choice.

"Yeah, why not?"

"Isn't that skirt wool? It's supposed to be over one hundred degrees again today."

"I don't care," Harry said.

"Well, I'm wearing this sundress and I'm not even going to take a sweater for the train, because it'll feel good to be a little cold today, if at all possible."

Walking through the crowded exhibit with Harry, I realized his whole outfit was in homage to the Scottish McQueen, who did entire collections in plaid. Complete strangers complimented Harry on his eccentric fashion-forward styling. I felt as I often did these days, like I was accompanying a celebrity designer who just happened to be my son.

We walked the six blocks from the Met to the subway on the shady side of the street, but my skin was wet with the dripping humidity. Underground, the subway platform felt like one of the lower levels of hell. I felt poached and was sure Harry might be feverish.

When the number 4 train arrived, I darted in to our air-conditioned escape. The car was practically empty, so I took the end spot in a row of three seats that faced the center. My back stuck to the orange molded plastic like a Post-It note, and I saw droplets form a band across Harry's forehead. I fanned myself with a postcard from the McQueen exhibit and offered one to Harry. We sat in the silence of cooling.

At the next stop, a man in his thirties boarded the train by himself. But instead of taking an open spot, he approached the seat on the other side of Harry. I heard him mumble something about Harry's black leather backpack-style purse, which occupied that seat. After the doors closed, he lifted Harry's bag, dropped it to the floor, and sat down. Without saying a word, Harry picked up his bag and set it on his lap. The man was still muttering when I glanced over to get a better look at him. But the way he was glaring at Harry startled me. Then I noticed a flash of metal in his left hand. He was holding a box cutter close to his thigh, flicking the blade in and out of its handle. I stopped breathing.

Oh my God . . . What do you think you're doing? I thought about jumping up to pull the cord of the emergency brake, but felt paralyzed. *What if I make a move and he decides to stab Harry?* I wanted only positive thoughts to kick in right about now, to imagine we were safe from harm and that nothing bad would happen. But the sharp blade and its proximity to Harry's body were all I could think about. Adrenaline rushed to my feet. I was terrified.

I nudged Harry with my right elbow. I wanted to signal him to change places with me. He stretched out the fingers of his left hand. I knew it was a cue not to say or do anything. Harry continued to stare straight ahead, refusing to respond to the homophobic killer I was convinced sat beside him. My heartbeat drummed in my ears, and I felt my stomach turn itself inside out.

Two stops later, the deranged man got off.

"Harry!" I gasped, clutching his arm. "That was so scary. Why didn't you move with me?"

"I figured he was just another crazy person," Harry said with a shrug. "Welcome to New York City, Mom."

"Well, I wanted to stop the train! I don't know how you could just sit there so calmly."

"I wanted to say, 'What the fuck are you looking at?' But I knew he was threatening me with that cutter."

"Do you think it was because you're wearing a skirt?" I asked.

"Indirectly, maybe. But he probably thought he had permission to harass me because I'm feminine."

I had felt helpless beside Harry. Now I was exhausted from the tension of sitting with my jaw clenched and shoulders stiffened up around my ears. Harry's eyes were closed and his head rested back against the wall of the train.

"Bubble of light, honey," I muttered. Then I took a deep breath. As much as I wanted to protect Harry in the bubble, I knew I couldn't control all the crazies in the world. Still, I wanted to choose positive thoughts, to expect the best out of situations, to trust I could navigate the unexpected and scary. Harry did this so beautifully. He had let his inner strength and confidence guide him. From the time he was bullied in fifth grade, he always seemed to handle himself so well. He inspired me to calm down and better manage my life.

I restrained myself from rubbing Harry's arm; I didn't want to wake him. Instead I looked up at the subway sign that had been in front of me all along. It read, "I ♥ New York more than ever." As the train lurched ahead from its last stop I knew I was moving forward, too.

Emily Ibarra

Harry performing at the Immaculate Contraception fundraiser, 2012

Epilogue:
The Night Jesus Wore Lace

Harry pulled out a chair opposite me at Shinju Sushi and took off his gray faux-fur coat.

"Honey, your resurrected Jesus last night was amazing!" I gushed. "The white lace robe over the floor-length lace gown was perfect. It looked like an outfit Prince would wear."

I knew I was speaking in superlatives, but Harry's performance at the "Immaculate Contraception" fundraiser for Planned Parenthood was the first drag appearance he'd invited me to attend.

"Thanks, Mom, I was pretty happy with how it all turned out."

"You were absolutely shining. And not just because of the blinking white lights in your gold crown of thorns, which also looked great, by the way."

Our waitress brought the pot of jasmine tea I had ordered and Harry poured out two cups full.

"I didn't realize that Amber Alert had such a following. So many people cheered when Nicole introduced you."

Harry closed his menu and laughed. "Mom, a lot of my friends from Wesleyan were there."

"Oh. Well, still, all eyes were on you. No one was even texting during your lip sync performance. And I loved the applause you got when your medley segued from 'Mercy' to 'Born to Die.'"

I looked at the handsome twenty-two-year-old across from me with the wavy reddish-brown hair, close-cropped beard, and tortoise-shell glasses. He appeared as confident and self-assured as he did when he was a boy. I felt flush with pride.

"All I can say is you've come a long way from the vampire geisha you were for Halloween when you were nine."

"I do love Halloween."

As I slid wooden chopsticks from a red paper wrapper, I thought about how clueless I was when I was trying to deal with my son's desire growing up to wear so-called girl clothes. I had definitely made some mistakes along the way. But looking back over my life as a parent, I felt like I'd made more right choices as Harry's mom than wrong ones. He'd reminded me of that while helping me pack up my personal files for the move to New York. He came across some instructions I had typed up for a new babysitter when he was just a year old.

"Listen to this," he'd said. "'I don't tell him "no" unless something isn't safe. If he's just getting into something, I usually try to distract him.'"

I told Harry I'd read somewhere that saying "no" all the time prevented toddlers from developing a sense of power over their own lives. When he asked if he could keep the eighteen-year-old document, I'd felt his appreciation of me ratchet up a notch. Still, there were the unfortunate decisions I had made, especially at Halloween. A twinge of bad-mother anxiety tightened in the back of my throat. I swallowed to relax.

"I know you don't remember me talking you into being Peter Pan instead of Wendy when you were two, but what about when you were four and wanted to be the Pink Power Ranger? Do you remember how you felt when I would only buy you the Blue Power Ranger costume?"

Harry was about to speak when the waitress returned with two miso soups.

Good. Give the boy some time to think.

"I just understood that I identified with the yellow and pink Power Rangers," Harry said, picking up his spoon. "There were three reasons. A, they had the best colors. B, they were girls. And C, the Pink Power Ranger was the only one with a skirt. That made her outfit better than anyone else's, which were pants. It wasn't as much about being a girl as it was about the clothes."

Of course . . . the clothes.

"And Kimberly," he continued, "that was the Pink Power Ranger, also had the best attitude."

"She did?"

"Yeah," Harry said, smiling. "I remember that the Power Rangers movie came out when I was in kindergarten, and she had the sassiest lines."

I grinned back at him. "So do you think Amber Alert has a little bit of Kimberly in her?"

"Definitely," Harry laughed. "Absolutely. She does, for sure."

"Thanks for filling me in about the skirt, Harry. You have no idea how bad I felt at the block party that night when your dad walked out in the pink and yellow satin caterpillar costume he rented on the way home from work."

"Mom, I didn't blame you for not letting me be the Pink Power Ranger. I didn't think you had the authority to override gender restrictions. I just figured you were enforcing the rules, end of discussion."

The word "rules" made me cringe. Was he saying I had been like my mother after all? Here, I thought I had come so far, that I had done such a good job with Harry. I knew I was a better mother than my mother, but maybe I had unwittingly modeled some aspects of her parenting.

"Oh, great," I said. "I fought my whole life not to be overbearing with you."

"I didn't think they were *your* rules, Mom. I thought they were rules the world imposed on us."

My shoulders relaxed along with a deep sigh. Leave it to perceptive little Harry to know more about life at four years old than I did as his mother.

"So, no emotional scarring?"

"No, none at all. I just believed what a lot of kids were led to believe: that girl costumes were for girls and boy costumes were for boys. There wasn't a lot out there that led kids to question that, except me."

Harry's pink and purple rhinestone-encrusted cell phone case began to vibrate on the table. He excused himself to take the call. I looked out the front window at a string of colored holiday lights. A rush of endorphins tickled my fingers and toes. I felt the euphoria that comes with a great Zumba workout and wanted to jump up dancing. Harry had just given me the best Christmas gift ever. He didn't blame me, or hold any grudge about my most ill-advised decision. And he didn't grow up believing he was bad or that there was something wrong with him or me.

When Harry put down the phone, I leaned across the table. "I want to tell you something."

He stared straight into my eyes.

"I think I learned more from you than you ever learned from me. When I wasn't sure how to help you find your place in the world, you taught me all I had to do was love you enough to get out of your way and let you be. You were my teacher, Harry."

He blushed and moved his right hand up to his chest, over his heart. "Oh, Mom, that's so sweet."

"It's true. And tonight was a reminder that I'm still learning."

Harry smiled at me with such love.

"Speaking of my education," I said, "I wanted to tell you I saw an interesting article last week about personal pronouns. Did you know about *zie* and *zir*?"

"Yeah, sure," Harry replied. "There's a whole Wikipedia page about them you can read if you want."

"I will check that out. Thanks."

"And I have to say I'm glad the conversation about gender pronouns is finally extending beyond college campuses."

"Me, too, honey," I said. I winced thinking how I'd tried to pigeonhole Harry before he even had an inkling of his sexuality. I had been so confused about gender identity and gender expression and what it all meant, so afraid I was going to screw up my only child, when clearly, looking at him now from across the table, he was a rock star.

"You're great, Mom."

"So are you," I said.

Harry felt I had done right by him and appreciated all of my efforts, and in the end, that's all any of us can do.

We said our goodbyes with a hug on the corner of Flatbush and Saint Marks Avenues. When I got back to my Brooklyn apartment, the home Harry had moved out of just two weeks before, I opened the door and noticed a speck of green glitter on the living room rug. It was an aspect of Harry's drag eye makeup that used to annoy me for making a complete mess of the bathroom sink. The neat freak in me would normally rush to pick it up and check for more, but tonight it made me smile, and I just let it be.

Harry and Ken at Clearwater Beach, Florida

Acknowledgments

I am deeply indebted to Harry for all I've learned from him, for everything he continues to teach me, and for giving me permission to write this book. My love for him knows no bounds.

So much thanks to Ken for saying at first mention that this was a story that needed to be told. I'm tremendously appreciative of his cover design that captures the essence of our kid and the love within these pages.

I'm very grateful to my agent, Claire Gerus, for believing in me and in this book. I also consider myself immensely fortunate to have had Raphael Kadushin as my editor. He assisted me in the developmental stages and then worked with me throughout the process on what was too much or not enough. My sincere thanks to the entire team at the University of Wisconsin Press for their enthusiasm, attention to detail, and kindness.

I don't know that I can ever express enough appreciation for Kimberlee Auerbach Berlin, my mentor and coach, who helped me find my voice, taught me how to tell stories that connected my mind with my heart, and pushed me beyond what I ever thought possible.

Big love and thanks to my siblings for letting me share moments from their lives that were also part of mine. I'm grateful to the rest of my wonderful family, too, for their start-to-finish encouragement and support.

Many, many thanks to: Debbie Borkin, Leah Borkin, Maura Donohue, Lily Drew, Jane Gallop, Mike Haertl, Katie Heil, Julie Hill, Emily Ibarra, Dean Jensen, Elvera Juraska, Randal Kleiser, Ruth Ku, Kevin McGeen, Leslee McGowan, Adam McKinney, Lizbeth Mitty, Michele Montijo, Cheryl Moskowitz, Peggy Mulloy, Judy Musil, Nik Nadolski, Anne Marie O'Farrell, Maren Siemers, Rick Stack, Alicia Torres, Chris Tuttle, Paul V. Vitagliano, Marissa Walsh, Liz Wasserman, Naomi Waxman, and Rachel Zarem.

Very special thanks to Tina Daniell and Patrick McGilligan for a perfect cup of tea.

Lastly, my gratitude to Héctor Torres for suggesting that I put the stories of my journey raising Harry into a book in the first place.

Resources for Families and Youth

Gender Spectrum (genderspectrum.org): Helps to create gender sensitive and inclusive environments for all children and teens.

It Gets Better Project (itgetsbetter.org): Communicates to lesbian, gay, bisexual, transgender, and queer/questioning youth around the world that it gets better, and creates and inspires the changes needed to make it better for them.

PFLAG (pflag.org): The nation's largest family and ally organization is committed to advancing equality and full societal affirmation of LGBTQ people through support, education, and advocacy.

The Parents Project (theparentsproject.com): A first-of-its-kind digital presence, inclusive of videos, advice, and resources, dedicated solely to helping parents understand their LGBTQ kids.

The Trevor Project (thetrevorproject.org): The leading national organization providing crisis intervention and suicide prevention services to LGBTQ young people.